EFFECTIVE ACADEMIC WRITING 1

THE PARAGRAPH

ALICE SAVAGE
North Harris College
Houston,

MASOU
Kingwoo
Kingwoo

Barbara,
These free samples
were sent to me, but
I thought you'd have
more use for them.
— Maryam 2095

OXFORD
UNIVERSITY PRESS

OXFORD
UNIVERSITY PRESS

198 Madison Avenue
New York, NY 10016 USA

Great Clarendon Street, Oxford OX2 6DP UK

Oxford University Press is a department of the University of Oxford.
It furthers the University's objective of excellence in research, scholarship,
and education by publishing worldwide in

Oxford New York

Auckland Cape Town Dar es Salaam Hong Kong Karachi
Kuala Lumpur Madrid Melbourne Mexico City Nairobi
New Delhi Shanghai Taipei Toronto

With offices in

Argentina Austria Brazil Chile Czech Republic France Greece
Guatemala Hungary Italy Japan Poland Portugal Singapore
South Korea Switzerland Thailand Turkey Ukraine Vietnam

OXFORD and OXFORD ENGLISH are registered trademarks of
Oxford University Press

Executive Publisher: Janet Aitchison
Senior Acquisitions Editor: Pietro Alongi
Editor: Rob Freire
Art Director: Maj-Britt Hagstead
Art Editor: Robin Fadool
Production Manager: Shanta Persaud
Production Controller: Eve Wong

ISBN-13: 978-0-19-430922-6 (STUDENT BOOK)
ISBN-10: 0-19-430922-3 (STUDENT BOOK)
ISBN-13: 978-0-19-430882-3 (ANSWER KEY)
ISBN-10: 0-19-430882-0 (ANSWER KEY)

Printed in Hong Kong

10 9 8 7 6 5 4 3 2 1

ACKNOWLEDGMENTS

Cover art:
Richard Diebenkorn
Ocean Park #122; 1980
oil and charcoal on canvas; 100 in. x 80 5/8 in. (254 cm x204.79 cm)
San Francisco Museum of Modern Art
Charles H. Land Familiar Foundation Fund purchase
© Estate of Richard Diebenkorn

Stills photography by:

Clockwise from top left: Purestock/Superstock: 2, Photo Edit Inc: David
Young-Wolff, 2; Punch Stock/Comstock: 2; Punch Stock: 2; Corbis: David
Turnley, 30; Photo Edit Inc.: David Young-Wolff, 52, Punch Stock/DGV: Carl
Roessler, 76; Superstock: Dwayne L. Harlan, 100; Bruce Coleman Inc.: G.
Krishnan, 122.

*We would like to thank the following for permission to reproduce these extracts and
adaptations of copyrighted material:*

p. 31. G.S. Sharat Chandra, excerpts from *Sari of the Gods*. Copyright © 1989
by G.S. Sharat Chandra. Reprinted with the permission of Coffee House
Press, Minneapolis, Minnesota; p. 101. Adapted from *Seattle* by Joel Rogers,
© 2006, with permission of Graphic Arts Books, an imprint of Graphic Arts
Center Publishing Company; p. 123. Excerpts from "The Green Mamba" from
Going Solo by Roald Dahl. Copyright © 1986 by Roald Dahl. Reprinted by
permission of Farrar, Straus and Giroux, LLC.

Acknowledgements

We would like to thank David Olsher, without whom we would never have started this project. We want to give a special thanks to the editorial team: Rob Freire, Kathleen Smith, Kenna Bourke, and Scott Allan Wallick for their insight and expertise, and Pietro Alongi for his endless positivity and support. We would also like to gratefully acknowledge the work of Susan Kesner Bland. Last but not least, our gratitude to the following reviewers for their contribution to the project: Sharon Allerson, East LA Community College; Frank Cronin, Austin Community College; Kieran Hilu, Virginia Tech; Peter Hoffman, LaGuardia Community College; Carla Nyssen, California State University Long Beach; Adrianne Ochoa; Mary O'Neill, North Virginia Community College; Maria Salinas, Del Mar College.

I would like to thank the administration, faculty, and staff of North Harris College for making it an inspiring place to work. I especially want to applaud the students of the ESL program. Your papers are full of delightful surprises and interesting insights. Thank you for allowing your work to be used to assist others. Finally, I wish to thank my husband, Masoud, and children Cyrus and Kaveh, for helping me balance work and home. I always look forward to seeing you at the end of the day. A.S.

I would like to express my appreciation to everyone at Kingwood College for creating a great environment for teaching and learning. I am especially grateful to the ESL faculty for their insightful suggestions and to the ESL students for their generosity in sharing their writing. Lastly, and most importantly, I would like to thank my wife Alice for working with me on this project and our sons Cyrus and Kaveh for adding so much color to our lives each and every day. M.S.

Contents

Unit 3: Example Paragraphs

Unit 4: Process Paragraphs

Unit 5: Opinion Paragraphs

Unit 6: Narrative Paragraphs

Appendices

Introduction

Effective Academic Writing is a three-book series intended to usher students into the world of academic writing. The goal of the series is to provide students and their teachers with a practical and efficient approach to learning the skills, strategies, and knowledge that are necessary for succeeding in content coursework. A parallel goal is to provide opportunities for students to explore their opinions, discuss their ideas, and share their experiences through written communication. By guiding budding writers through the experience of composing various types of paragraphs and short papers, we hope to provide students with the tools and the confidence necessary for college success.

The Paragraph

Book 1 of *Effective Academic Writing, The Paragraph*, introduces students at the high-beginning to low-intermediate level to the academic paragraph. The first unit provides a review of sentence structure and an introduction to developing and formatting an academic paragraph. Each of the following five units then addresses a particular rhetorical mode and provides user-friendly guidance to mastering the form. The book also offers numerous opportunities for practicing relevant grammar points. All grammar presentations and practice are correlated to *Grammar Sense 1*.

Book 1 contains several features designed to support students in developing the skills that they need for college writing:

- Each unit contains an authentic text to provide ideas and context for the assignment.
- At strategic points in the unit, students read and analyze authentic student paragraphs to see how other students have written on the same or similar topics.
- Each unit contains concise and effective language presentations designed to develop students' understanding of rhetorical modes and to improve their grammatical accuracy.
- Each unit offers useful writing outlines so that students can structure their writing and internalize the practice.
- Each unit offers collaborative learning activities allowing students to work together and share ideas.
- At relevant points in the unit, editing exercises and editing checklists are provided so that students can refine their writing.
- Timed writing activities come at the close of each unit to prepare students for in-class writing.
- A series of learner-friendly appendices are provided at the back of the book to encourage student independence. A glossary of common grammar terms for student reference is included.

Unit Organization

Each unit introduces a theme and a writing task and then guides the writer through a five-part process of gathering ideas, organizing an outline, drafting, revising, and editing. As students write, they practice specific skills and put language knowledge to work to produce a paragraph that follows academic conventions. The rhetorical and language-related goals of the unit are identified on the opener page.

Part 1

Part 1 opens with an image to spark interest as students begin thinking about the topic. This is followed by a short authentic text. Students answer questions about the text that will help them connect the writer's ideas to their own knowledge and experience. They then move on to a freewriting activity, an unstructured writing task in which they can explore the topic without worrying about organization or grammar.

Part 2

In Part 2 students are introduced to a specific rhetorical mode. They begin by brainstorming ideas and vocabulary that they will use to write their paragraph. They then learn about rhetorical organizational features and read and analyze a student paragraph. Finally, students produce an outline for the paragraph they will write later in the unit.

Part 3

In Part 3 students develop the ideas from their outline and produce a first draft. This part opens with a second student paragraph for students to analyze. As they answer questions about the second student model, students review the organizational features learned in Part 2. They are then introduced to specific, level-appropriate language points that will help students shape and structure their writing. Students now write their first draft and, using a peer-review checklist, check each other's writing for organization and clarity of ideas.

Part 4

In Part 4 students edit their writing and produce a final draft. This part focuses on particular grammar trouble spots relevant to the theme and the rhetorical style presented in the unit. Following the concise language presentation, students complete practice exercises to help them develop their grammar skills and build confidence. Students then move on to editing their own writing, and produce a final draft.

Part 5

The final part of the unit is titled "Putting It All Together." This is the summary of the other parts of the unit. Through a series of skill exercises, students review the points covered in Parts 1–4. They are then given the opportunity to write a timed paragraph using a similar rhetorical focus, but on a different topic. Guidelines for using their time efficiently are suggested. This part also provides students with a comprehensive checklist to review what they have written. The unit closes with suggested tasks for future writing that can be used for more practice.

Unit 1

The Sentence and the Paragraph

Unit Goals

Rhetorical focus:
- paragraph organization
- formatting a paragraph
- unity and coherence in a paragraph

Language focus:
- simple sentence structure
- capitalization and end punctuation
- fragments and run-on sentences

| Exercise 1 | **Thinking about the topic** |

Discuss the pictures with a partner.

- Look at the people writing. What kind of writing is each person doing?
- Are they writing for others or for themselves?
- What other kinds of writing can you think of?
- What kind of writing do you usually do?

Rhetorical Focus

The Paragraph

A paragraph is a group of sentences about a topic. In this book, you will learn how to organize and write the following kinds of paragraphs.

- In a **descriptive paragraph** the writer describes a person, a place, or a thing.

- In an **example paragraph** the writer explains a topic by giving examples.

- In a **process paragraph** the writer explains how to do something step by step.

- In an **opinion paragraph** the writer expresses his or her feelings, ideas, and opinions about a topic.

- In a **narrative paragraph** the writer tells a story.

Formatting a Paragraph

Margins

A paragraph must have a margin on the right and a margin on the left. This means that the paragraph begins 1 inch or 1 1/4 inches from the edge of the paper.

Spacing

A paragraph should be double-spaced.

Indenting

The first sentence of a paragraph must be indented. This means that it begins five spaces in from the left margin. Indenting shows the reader that a new paragraph is beginning. On a computer, you can indent with the Tab key.

Connected Sentences

The sentences in a paragraph should follow each other. It is not a paragraph if every sentence begins on a new line. A well-supported paragraph has at least 5 sentences and often more.

Title

A paragraph by itself usually has a title. This is one word or a group of words that tells what the topic is.

Read the paragraph. Then label the formatting elements of the paragraph. Use the words in the box.

a. margin   b. double spacing   c. indent   d. title

1. ____ ⟶   **Red**

2. ____ ⟶   I love the color red. No other color symbolizes so many different

emotions and experiences. Life would be very boring without the color

3. ____ ⟶   red. Fires would not burn in the same way. The sunset would not be

interesting, and blood would not be so surprisingly beautiful. Red is

powerful when it appears in nature, and it is also powerful when it

4. ____   appears in our emotions. Red is love. Red is anger. Red is beauty. I

like to live life in a strong way, so I think I will always admire the

color red.

In Part 2 you will …

• learn about paragraph organization

PART 2

Developing a Paragraph

Rhetorical Focus

Paragraph Organization

A typical paragraph has a topic sentence, supporting sentences, and a concluding sentence.

- The **topic sentence** introduces the topic and tells what the writer will say about the topic.

- The sentences that follow further explain and support the topic sentence. They are called **supporting sentences**.

- The **concluding sentence** often repeats the information in the topic sentence in a different way.

| Exercise 1 | **Reading a student paragraph** |

Read the paragraph below and note the topic sentence, supporting sentences, and concluding sentence. What was it that scared the barefoot boy?

Barefoot Boy

topic sentence

I had a scary experience when I was a young boy. One evening while my parents were eating dinner, I was playing barefoot in the yard with my toys. Even now I still remember the perfume of the flowers and the moisture of the grass. While I was sitting on the grass and playing with a truck, I looked up at the sky, and my attention was distracted by the beauty of the stars. Then I felt something cold and smooth slide over my feet. I stayed perfectly still, but I looked down at my feet. Then I saw a snake slowly slithering over my toes. I felt terrible and afraid, so my heart beat very fast. After the snake moved away, I screamed to my parents for help, and they captured the snake and took it away. The experience frightened me, and I never went outside barefoot again.

supporting sentences

concluding sentence

Analyzing the student paragraph

Examine the organization of the paragraph by answering the questions.

1. What is the topic sentence? Write it below.

   _____

2. How many supporting sentences are there? _____

3. In your opinion, do the supporting sentences explain the topic
   sentence? _____

4. Write the concluding sentence below.

   _____

5. Does the concluding sentence repeat the information in the topic sentence in
   a new way? _____

Rhetorical Focus

The Topic Sentence

The topic sentence is usually the first or second sentence in a
paragraph. It introduces a new idea. It presents the topic and explains
what the writer will say about the topic. This explanation is called the
controlling idea.

Read the following topic sentences. In each one, the topic is *my
friend*. The controlling ideas explain what the writer will say about
the topic. These controlling ideas tell the reader what to expect in the
supporting sentences.

| topic | controlling idea |

My friend is an honest person.

My friend is the funniest person I know.

My friend has a terribly dangerous job.

A topic sentence must not be a simple fact or a specific detail. The
controlling idea must say something about the topic that can then be
supported, developed, or demonstrated in the supporting sentences.
The controlling idea must also not be too general, or the topic
sentence will be unclear.

A surprise party is a kind of party.   (*too general*)

There were 14 guests at my surprise birthday party.   (*too specific*)

My classmates gave me an unforgettable surprise party for my 18th birthday.

The last topic sentence is effective because it introduces the topic
and has a controlling idea that can be developed in the supporting
sentences. The paragraph will probably tell the story of the party.

Exercise 3   Identifying topics and controlling ideas

In each topic sentence below, circle the topic and underline the controlling idea.

1. (Hiking) is the best way to explore nature closely.

2. My uncle had a frightening experience as a young man.

3. Text messaging has become popular among teenagers.

4. Effective time management requires four easy steps.

5. Every college student should take a computer course.

Exercise 4   Identifying effective topic sentences

In each sentence below, circle the topic and underline the controlling idea. If the sentence does not contain an effective controlling idea, write an ✗ in the blank. For the effective topic sentences, write what you think the supporting sentences will be about.

1. _____ (My doctor) is very kind to his patients.
   The writer will give examples of ways in which his doctor is kind to patients.

2. _____ Fried rice is easy to prepare if you follow some simple steps.
   _____

3. _____ I am going to write about my country.
   _____

4. _____ I had an adventure in the jungle last year.
   _____

5. _____ Video games are not bad for children.
   _____

Exercise 5   Writing topic sentences

Use each word or phrase below to write a topic sentence with a controlling idea. Then share your sentences with a partner.

1. Pets
   Pets are good companions for older people.

2. A first date
   _____

3. A terrible teacher
   _____

4. Tennis
   _____

Supporting Sentences

Supporting sentences add information about the topic and the controlling idea. Supporting sentences can include **definitions, explanations**, and **examples**. Read the topic sentence below. Then study the types of supporting sentences that might follow it.

topic		controlling idea

Young people are too dependent on computers.

Supporting definition

Dependency on computers means that young people cannot perform the normal tasks and functions of daily life without them.

Supporting explanation

In the old days, people memorized important information, but today's youth rely on their computers, cell phones, and PDA's to do assignments, record numbers, and save important information. As a result, they can find themselves unprepared in an emergency such as an electrical blackout. Once their batteries die, these people will not be able communicate.

Supporting example

For example, I do all my schoolwork on my computer. When my computer crashed last week, I lost my only draft of an essay that was due the next day. As a result, I got a bad grade.

Exercise 6   Identifying topic sentences and supporting sentences

For each set of sentences, write *TS* next to the topic sentence. Write *SS* next to the supporting sentences.

1. _SS_ a. Mosquitoes are attracted to heat.

   _SS_ b. Mosquitoes will fly several miles to find food.

   _SS_ c. Only the female mosquito bites.

   _TS_ d. Mosquitoes are interesting insects.

2. ____ a. One of my hobbies is listening to international music.

   ____ b. I have a large collection of world music recordings.

   ____ c. My friends and I like to introduce each other to new international artists we discover.

   ____ d. I enjoy going to concerts by musicians from different countries.

3. ____ a. I like the way people decorate their homes and stores.

____ b. I enjoy going shopping in cold weather.

____ c. I enjoy the parties and celebrations of the winter holiday.

____ d. I really like the winter holidays.

4. ____ a. My new apartment has big closets.

____ b. My new apartment is perfect for my roommate and me.

____ c. My new apartment is close to school and work.

____ d. My new apartment is not too expensive for students.

Rhetorical Focus

The Concluding Sentence

The concluding, or final, sentence of a paragraph usually reminds the reader of the topic and controlling idea of the paragraph. The concluding sentence restates the main idea.

Topic sentence

I love the color red.

Concluding sentence

I like to live life in a strong way, so I think I will always admire the color red.

In addition to restating the main idea, the concluding sentence may:

• warn the reader.

   If you do not follow these steps, you may not get the grade that you want.

• make a prediction.

   The automotive industry will change, and soon everyone will be driving pollution-free cars.

• give an opinion about the topic.

   Some people might disagree, but I think lamb is the best meat for grilling.

Sometimes writers signal the concluding sentence by using the phrase *In conclusion*.

In conclusion, learning a second language has many advantages.

Identifying supporting sentences and concluding sentences

Read the topic sentences below. Write *SS* next to the three supporting sentences and write *CS* next to the concluding sentence.

1. The best way to see San Francisco is by walking.

    CS a. When you explore San Francisco by foot, you can experience all the city has to offer.

    SS b. When you walk, you experience the different smells of the restaurants, the plants and sometimes the ocean.

    SS c. You can stop and look in the windows of shops or sit on a bench for a short while and look at interesting people.

    SS d. In a car or a bus, you cannot stop easily if you see something interesting because parking is difficult.

2. An egg taco takes only five minutes to make.

    _____ a. Your delicious egg taco is ready to eat in just a few minutes.

    _____ b. Heat a flour tortilla in a small amount of water.

    _____ c. Scramble two eggs with a little salt and pepper.

    _____ d. When the eggs are done, slide them into the warm tortilla and fold it over.

3. My paper is late because something happened to my computer.

    _____ a. I was almost finished writing my paper, and I was checking it for errors.

    _____ b. Suddenly, my computer screen went blank, and the power was gone.

    _____ c. The accident made me lose many hours of work, so I could not turn in my essay on time.

    _____ d. Later, I learned that a squirrel got on the power line and disrupted the electricity.

4. I enjoy the riverwalk in San Antonio.

    _____ a. The riverwalk is lower than the streets of the city.

    _____ b. You can walk down stairs to a canal with a stone path and plants on each side.

    _____ c. There are many shops, restaurants and hotels along the path.

    _____ d. The riverwalk is a pleasant place to spend an afternoon or evening in San Antonio.

Examining concluding sentences

Circle the word that best describes each of the concluding sentences below.

1. If you follow these steps, you will never lose your keys again.

    a. (prediction)　　　　　b. opinion　　　　　c. warning

2. Students who are not careful with credit cards can go into debt quickly.

    a. prediction　　　　　b. opinion　　　　　c. warning

3. Venice, Italy, is the most beautiful city in the world.

    a. prediction　　　　　b. opinion　　　　　c. warning

4. You will be able to produce a beautiful paper crane with only a little bit of practice.

    a. prediction　　　　　b. opinion　　　　　c. warning

5. There are many reasons why movie stars make poor politicians.

    a. prediction　　　　　b. opinion　　　　　c. warning

6. The desert is a beautiful but dangerous place to hike, so do your research and take time to prepare carefully.

    a. prediction　　　　　b. opinion　　　　　c. warning

In Part 3 you will …

• learn about unity and coherence in paragraphs.

PART 3

Unity and Coherence

Good academic writers follow specific steps to make sure their writing is both clear and accurate. They gather, organize, and develop ideas. They write drafts, sometimes two or more. When they revise each draft, good writers look for unity, coherence, and grammatical problems.

Rhetorical Focus

Unity within a Paragraph

A paragraph must have unity. A paragraph has unity when all the sentences support a single idea.

- The paragraph must have one controlling idea in the topic sentence. Otherwise the paragraph loses focus.

- The supporting sentences must support or explain the controlling idea with examples, details, steps, or definitions. Otherwise, the paragraph will not be about one single idea.

- The concluding sentence should restate the idea in the topic sentence. Otherwise the main idea might not be clear.

Topic sentence

My friend Macarena is generous.

Supporting sentences

She often lets travelers stay in her home. She has hosted many students temporarily. She sends money to her family in Chile every month to help them with their bills. She always brings flowers or food to her friends when they are sick or have a need.

Concluding sentence

Macarena is one of the most generous people I know.

Note that all the sentences are about Macarena's generosity. A sentence about the way she looks or about her job will not support the unity of the paragraph unless it somehow relates to Macarena's generosity.

Reading a student paragraph

Read the paragraph. Where did the pink sheep come from?

The Pink Sheep

Many years ago, a special gift came to me in an interesting way. When I was a small boy, I enjoyed playing in my garden. One day, I found a hole in the wall of my garden. It was near the ground, so I could not see through the hole, but I knew that behind the wall was my neighbor's garden. Who made that hole? I felt really interested, so I used rocks to make the hole wider. One day, when I was trying to break through the wall, I noticed a small hand appear from the hole. The hand was holding a rubber sheep. It was pink and it had wide eyes. I caught that rubber sheep. Then I pushed my favorite wooden truck through the hole to give to that child on the other side. Sometimes I bought toys with my lucky New Year money. A long time later, when I was old enough to go out, I went around the corner to find the child who gave me that special gift, but nobody was in that house. My neighbor said that a girl used to live there, and she was the same age as me. I never found her, but her gift has a special meaning for me.

Analyzing a student paragraph for unity

Examine the organization of the paragraph by answering the questions below. Then compare your answers with a partner.

1. Circle the topic and underline the controlling idea.

2. After you read the controlling idea, what did you expect the supporting ideas to explain. Write your answer in your own words.

   _____

   _____

3. One sentence in the paragraph is off-topic and does not support the unity of the paragraph. Draw a line through it.

4. Why does this sentence hurt the unity of the paragraph? Write your explanation below.

   _____

   _____

Recognizing unity in supporting sentences

Read the following topic sentences. Put a check (✓) next to each sentence below that supports the topic sentence.

1. I am an organized person.

    ✓ a. My desk is always neat and tidy.

    ✓ b. I have a system for organizing my papers, and I can always find what I need.

    ____ c. I feel uncomfortable when I am in a strange environment.

    ✓ d. My friends always want me to help them put their closets in order.

2. Twenty questions is an easy game to play when you are traveling.

    ____ a. The person who is "it" must think of a person, place, or object.

    ____ b. Sometimes people travel by car, and sometimes by train or airplane.

    ____ c. It is very important to travel with people that you get along with.

    ____ d. The other players take turns asking questions that can only be answered with "yes" or "no."

3. Tea and coffee are very different from each other.

    ____ a. Coffee has more caffeine than tea does.

    ____ b. Coffee and tea both have caffeine.

    ____ c. People enjoy tea and coffee during social occasions.

    ____ d. Tea is much more common around the world than coffee is.

4. In my opinion, people spend too much money on cars.

    ____ a. Some drivers spend a fourth of their income for a car payment, which is unnecessary.

    ____ b. Cars do not increase in value, so they are not a great investment.

    ____ c. Car companies are always looking for ways to make vehicles safer on the road.

    ____ d. People who do not pay cash must also pay interest, so they lose even more money.

5. It is easy to get a sports injury.

    ____ a. Many people enjoy sports.

    ____ b. Runners often have problems with their ankles and knees.

    ____ c. Basketball players can break their fingers or get knocked over by another player.

    ____ d. Many people make the simple mistake of joining a gym, and then they never go there to exercise.

6. My city is famous because of its architecture.

     ____ a. We have ancient red-tiled buildings around the main square.

     ____ b. The restaurants near the beach serve great seafood.

     ____ c. It has expensive tree-lined boulevards with beautiful limestone buildings and monuments.

     ____ d. A famous university is located on the side of a mountain.

Exercise 4 **Editing for unity**

Read the paragraph below. Cross out the two sentences that are not about the controlling idea.

Life in a New Place

I am a Thai girl living in the U.S., and there are many adjustments that I must make. First of all, I must get used to a new kind of food. I am learning to eat a lot of hamburgers because they are not expensive and they are easy to buy. The people are different and I am learning to meet new foreign friends. For example, two of my new friends are from Pakistan. Pakistan is also an interesting country to visit. The weather requires another kind of adjustment. Some days, it is hot just as in my country, but on other days it is cold and this is very strange for me. I came to the U.S. to study and I enjoy my classes and my teachers. I am adjusting to the U.S. in many ways, but it is not a problem for me because I like to know about different places and people.

Exercise 5 **Developing unity**

Write two supporting sentences for each of the following topic sentences. Then exchange books with a partner and check your partner's sentences for unity.

1. Computers are useful in many ways.

    _____

    _____

2. There are certain characteristics that I always look for in a good restaurant.

    _____

    _____

3. When I want to look nice for a party, I follow a few simple steps.

_____

_____

4. There are activities in a park for family members of all ages.

_____

_____

5. There are many ways to show respect to older people.

_____

_____

6. When you are going camping, there are some things you should always take with you.

_____

_____

Rhetorical Focus

Coherence within a Paragraph

A paragraph must also have coherence. This means that the supporting details are organized so that information that goes together appears together.

Writers often use **time, space,** or **order of importance** to present the supporting information in a paragraph coherently. The following example is organized by space.

When you drive into the airport, you will see many signs for the different terminals. After you pass the signs, you will drive over a hill. The airport is on the other side of the hill. On your right, you will see the international terminal. This terminal is two stories tall. The front is all glass. On the left, you will see the domestic terminals…

Read the paragraphs below. Then circle the word that best describes the way the paragraph is organized.

Paragraph 1

My favorite restaurant is in an old house. It is very convenient because it is in my neighborhood. We can drive, or if the evening is pleasant, we can walk. It has a nice atmosphere and friendly service. We know some of the waiters and waitresses so we enjoy talking to them because they ask us about our children. We especially like the decorations. The walls are soft yellow, and candles and fresh flowers are on the tables inside and outside. Finally, the food is excellent. The cook is the owner and he makes delicious dishes with fresh ingredients. We always enjoy our meals.

Time   **Space**   **Order of importance**

Paragraph 2

My favorite restaurant is in an old house. My husband and I enjoy eating there on summer evenings. We usually walk from our house so we can enjoy our neighbors' gardens and get a little bit of exercise. The afternoon sun shines through the trees but it is not too bright. We arrive at dusk, and if we are lucky, we can sit outside. The waiter brings a basket of warm bread and a cold drink. We have an appetizer or a salad while the sun goes down. Then the waiter lights the candles while we enjoy the main course. By the time we finish desert, it is night time. We walk home slowly, feeling full but happy in the moonlight.

Time   **Space**   **Order of importance**

Read the following paragraphs. Which one has better coherence? What is the pattern of organization?

Paragraph 1

Soccer brings the world together in many ways. During the World Cup, people from all over the world are tuned in. If they can not see it in person, they watch it on television. Many countries participate in the world cup. People learn about the teams from different countries, and they learn something about those countries. When people are watching the World Cup, they do not care if the game is on at four a.m. in their country. They will stay up to watch it. They learn about the flags from different countries because they will see the fans.

Paragraph 2

The best way to meet new friends is to take a class. First, all the people in a class have something in common. They all want to learn about the subject, so there is something to talk about. Second, everyone sees each other every time the class meets, so there are many opportunities to get to know others. Third, there are often activities and group projects so students can work together, and this is the best way to get to know people. By the end of the class, it is hard not to know your classmates.

In Part 4 you will …

- learn about simple sentence structure.
- learn about end punctuation and capitalization.
- learn about fragments and run-on sentences.

PART 4

Editing Your Writing

Language Focus

Simple Sentence Structure

A sentence is a statement that expresses a complete idea. Sentences form the building blocks of written communication. They include affirmative statements, negative statements, and questions. A complete sentence must have a **subject** and a **verb**.

Subject

The subject tells who or what the sentence is about. Sometimes the subject is singular, and sometimes it is plural.

Fatima smiled. *(singular subject)*
Siblings fight. *(plural subject)*

Subjects can be more than one word.

Lois and Peter have eight children.
The hungry kittens ran to their mother.

Verb

The verb refers to an action or a state. It indicates tense or time. Two common tenses are present and past.

Jared **sings**. *(present tense)*
Ducks **walked** across the street. *(past tense)*

A sentence can have more than one verb.
My brother **studied** hard and **earned** a degree in economics.

Exercise 1   **Identifying subjects and verbs**

Underline the subject and circle the verb(s) in each sentence.

1. My mother (raised) seven children.

2. She cooked and cleaned all day long.

3. My father and his brother have a small business.

4. My three sisters live in Vietnam.

5. I help my aunt during the day and go to school in the evening.

6. My parents bought a new car.

Answer each question below in a complete sentence. When you finish, exchange books with your partner. Then underline the subject and circle the verb in each of your partner's sentences.

1. What sports do you enjoy?

    I enjoy soccer and tennis.

2. Where do you live?

    _____

3. What do you like to do on the weekends?

    _____

4. Where do you study?

    _____

5. What kind of food do you like?

    _____

6. Who do you enjoy spending time with?

    _____

Language Focus

Punctuation and Capitalization

- The first word in a sentence is always capitalized.
  The wedding lasts for several days.

- A complete sentence can end in a period.
  A good speech begins with a joke.

- A question ends with a question mark.
  Do you enjoy learning about the world?

- Occasionally, writers use an exclamation mark to give emphasis to a sentence.
  I looked down and sliding across my bare foot was a giant green mamba!

Read the paragraph. In each sentence, underline the subject and circle the verb(s). Then draw a box around each end punctuation.

Summer by the Sea

<u>My favorite memory</u> (is) about my family. It happened a long time ago before my brother got married and moved out. My parents had seven children. All seven of us piled in one car for a summer holiday by the beach. We traveled in that crowded car for two days! Finally we arrived at a small house near the beach. It had one big room with many beds and an other room for eating and cooking. The kids spent all day outside. We played together in the water. Sometimes, my mother made a picnic dinner. We sat on the sand to eat and watch the sun go down. One night we brought out blankets and slept by the water. I loved that time. We talked and looked at the stars until late at night. This wonderful summer holiday was the best time of my life.

Language Focus

Fragments

Every sentence must have a subject and a verb and express a complete idea. A sentence that is missing a subject or a verb is incomplete. It is called a **fragment**.

Incorrect	**Correct**
I like Minneapolis. Is a clean city. *(subject is missing)*	I like Minneapolis. **It** is a clean city.
They successful. *(verb is missing)*	They **are** successful.

Decide whether each fragment below is missing a subject or a verb. Then rewrite it so that it is correct.

1. Some food very spicy.

   Some food is very spicy.

2. Corn my favorite vegetable.

   _____

3. Is very bright in the afternoon.

   _____

4. Takes a nap for two or three hours.

   _____

5. Eats rice.

   _____

6. There flowers in the market.

   _____

Language Focus

Run-on Sentences

Two sentences that run together without correct punctuation between them are called **run-on sentences**. One way to correct a run-on sentence is to put a period between the sentences. Another way is to add a comma and a connecting word.

Incorrect	Correct
I received a letter it was from my sister. (*no punctuation between two sentences*)	I received a letter. It was from my sister. (*period added between the sentences*)
They laughed, I felt better. (*comma alone between two sentences*)	They laughed, and I felt better. (*connecting word added*)

Identifying and correcting run-on sentences

Correct the following run-on sentences by rewriting them on the blanks below.

1. I am a full-time student, I live in a great apartment near campus.
   I am a full-time student, and I live in a great apartment near campus.

2. There are mice living underneath my house they make a lot of noise at night.

   _____

3. I used to eat rice and vegetables for breakfast now I eat cereal and milk.

   _____

4. I do not drive, I ride the bus.

   _____

5. I am saving money for a bicycle I also want to buy a camera.

   _____

Exercise 6 **Editing for fragments and run-on sentences**

Correct the three fragments and two run-on errors in the following paragraph. Do not forget to use appropriate punctuation and capitalization.

My Hotel Job

My mother's cousin owned a hotel, and I worked there as a young man. I enjoyed this work very much. Met many interesting people. One time a family came to stay in the hotel. They a daughter, she was my age. We met often and talked about our lives. I invited her to my house to meet my family. She told us about her life in the United States. We shared our customs with her. Later my mother told me something unforgettable. She said, "I know that you are going to live in America." My mother a very smart woman, she was right. I came to America to search for my friend. I am still looking.

In Part 5 you will …

- review the elements of a paragraph.
- review unity and coherence.
- review correcting fragments and run-on sentences.

PART 5

Putting It All Together

Exercise 1   **Identifying the elements of a paragraph**

Read the paragraph. Then label the formatting elements of the
paragraph. Use the words in the box.

a. margin	b. double spacing	c. indent	d. title

1. ____   → **My Grandfather the Baker**

2. ____   → My grandfather has a lot of respect in our community. He is the
owner of a bakery called "The Family Bread Factory." The bakery has

3. ____   → been his profession since he was young. He started working there at
the age of 13. He learned many recipes. The most delicious and secret
recipe uses oatmeal and other ingredients that only he knows. This

4. ____   bread made him famous. Nowadays he makes some bread only once in
a while because his legs bother him, and he gets tired easily. Instead,
he sits at a table, and the people of the town come to buy bread and to
pay their respects. Everyone admires him very much because he is an
honest and hardworking man.

Exercise 2   **Identifying topic sentences and supporting sentences**

For each set of sentences, write *TS* next to the topic sentence that
states the topic and provides a controlling idea. Write *SS* next to the
supporting sentences.

1. ____ a. The calendars are different.

   ____ b. The weekend starts on Friday instead of Saturday.

   ____ c. The time is different because my country does not follow Greenwich time.

   ____ d. There are some very specific differences between my part of the
   world and the western countries.

2. ____ a. I was traveling to Los Angeles to visit my cousin.

   ____ b. My plane was delayed, so I was stuck at the airport.

   ____ c. I experienced a strange coincidence last year.

   ____ d. I heard my math teacher from my old hometown calling my name.

3. ____ a. I like several things about my English class.

____ b. I am meeting many new friends from different countries.

____ c. Every day, I learn new words, and I keep them in a notebook.

____ d. Sometimes we play games and laugh during the class time.

4. ____ a. You can use the Internet to find a great deal of information, but if you do not have the right skills, you can waste a lot of time.

____ b. The Internet can be incredibly useful if you know how to use it.

____ c. There are opportunities to buy and sell products on the Internet, but you have to know the proper way to send money.

____ d. The Internet is a good place to find a job for people who know how to use search engines.

Exercise 3   Evaluating concluding sentences

Read the paragraphs below. Then read the concluding sentences that follow and decide which one works best. Copy the sentence you choose into the paragraph.

There They Are!

I feel happy whenever I am standing beside a train track because I am waiting for someone who is close to me. I was the youngest child in my family, so my older brothers and sisters left home before I did. However, they always returned for vacations and holidays. My mother and father and I were always at the train station to greet them. I enjoyed the smell of the train and the roaring noise it made as the big black engine pulled into the station. I would jump up and down trying to see while everyone crowded around the doors. "There they are!" my mother would cry. I would run to jump into the arms of my beloved brother or sister. _____

_____

a. In conclusion, I always had an enjoyable visit with my brothers and sisters.

b. In conclusion, my whole family likes train stations.

c. Now I am an adult, but I still feel joy when I go to the train station to meet someone I love.

A Wise Shopper

A consumer can save a lot of money by shopping wisely. This means he is always looking for sales and collecting coupons, but it also means the person is not a compulsive shopper. In other words, the wise consumer does his research and makes a plan so that he knows what he is looking for. He is not tempted by attractive products that are not necessary. Sometimes he goes home without purchasing anything. He might think he wasted his time but he knows he did not waste his money. _____

_____

a. In conclusion, a compulsive shopper can never be a wise shopper.
b. In conclusion, a wise shopper also keeps a budget so that he knows how much he can spend.
c. In conclusion, a wise shopper finds ways to save money on the price and to avoid buying what he does not need.

Exercise 4   **Editing a paragraph**

Read the paragraph below. Cross out the two sentences that do not support the topic sentence.

My Red Couch

I acquired a new couch in an interesting way. I was walking to the bus stop, and I saw a yard sale. The family was selling a beautiful but heavy red couch at a very good price. I really liked the couch, and I wanted to buy it. However, there was a problem. I did not have a truck, and my apartment was five blocks away. Suddenly, I saw my classmate across the street. She usually sat next to me in a computer class. I told her my problem, and she offered to help. Then I paid for the couch and my friend and I carried it down the street. When we got tired, we sat down to rest on the sidewalk. Finally, we brought it to my door, and my neighbor helped carry it upstairs. I really like to buy old things because I live in an old building. It was a funny day for me, and I like to remember this day whenever I come home and see my beautiful red couch.

Exercise 5 Identifying subjects and verbs

Underline the subject and circle the verb(s) in each sentence.

1. My classmate drinks hot chocolate.

2. We lived in Lima.

3. Hong Kong has many interesting neighborhoods.

4. My brother eats rice and drinks milk at every meal.

Exercise 6 Practicing with end punctuation.

Add the correct end punctuation to the following sentences.

1. How do men and women meet each other_____

2. When I got home, there were candles and fresh flowers everywhere_____

3. He was late to his own birthday party_____

4. The guests danced Merengue and Salsa_____

Exercise 7 Identifying and correcting fragments

Decide whether each fragment below is missing a subject or a verb. Then rewrite it correctly.

1. Suddenly fell down.

   _____

2. Has a tropical climate.

   _____

3. I walking beside the lake with my best friend.

   _____

4. Was an important day for me.

   _____

Correct the following run-on sentences by rewriting them on the
blanks below.

1. We watched a movie it was about a dinosaur that lost its mother.

    _____

2. We have a harvest moon festival every year in our city, there are parades and
    kiosks with noodle soup and other delicious food.

    _____

3. I had to stop going to school for a while, my father wanted me to help him
    with his business.

    _____

4. Rice pudding is delicious and easy to make it is great for parties, too.

    _____

Descriptive Paragraphs

Unit Goals

Rhetorical focus:
- descriptive organization

Language focus:
- using specific language
- using adjectives in descriptive writing
- using *be* to define and describe

PART 1

Stimulating Ideas

In a descriptive paragraph, the writer uses words that create an image and help the reader see, touch, feel, smell, or taste the topic that he or she is describing.

Exercise 1 **Thinking about the topic**

Discuss the picture with a partner.

- How is the woman dressed?
- Where is she?
- Have you ever seen someone dressed this way? If so, where?

Exercise 2 **Reading about the topic**

Prapulla is a young Indian bride. She and her husband, Shekar, are moving to New York, where he has a job with a U.S. company. Prapulla must decide how she will dress in her new country: in western pants and skirts, or in a sari, the traditional dress for Indian women. Why is the sari so special to Prapulla?

Sari of the Gods

En route to New York on the **jumbo**, Shekar had discreetly opened up the conversation about what she'd wear once they were in America. At the mention of skirts she had flared up so defiantly he had to leave the seat. For Prapulla, it was not convenience but **convention** that made the difference. She had always **prized** her saris, especially on the occasions when she wore her wedding sari with its blue, **hand-spun silk** and its silver **border** on which images of the gods had been **embroidered**.

…

She remembered the day she had shopped for the sari. It had been a week before her wedding. The entire family had gone to the silk **bazaar** and spent the day looking for the perfect one. They had at last found it in the only hand-spun sari shop in the market. The merchant had explained that the weaver who had knitted the gods into its border had died soon after, taking his **craft** with him. This was his last sari, his parting gift to some lucky bride.

Sharat Chandra, G. S. *Sari of the Gods*. Minneapolis: Coffee House Press, 1989.

en route: on the way
jumbo: a large airplane
convention: a traditional way of behaving or doing something
prized: considered something very valuable
hand-spun: woven by hand
silk: an expensive, soft, smooth fabric

border: the edge of something
embroidered: decorated by sewing with small stitches
bazaar: an open market with many shops and stalls
craft: ability or skill

Exercise 3 | Understanding the text

Write *T* for true or *F* for false for each statement.

____ 1. Prapulla went shopping for her wedding sari with her family.

____ 2. Prapulla's wedding sari was made by hand.

____ 3. Prapulla's wedding sari was white.

____ 4. The man who wove Prapulla's wedding sari told her she was lucky.

____ 5. The sari was the last one in the store.

Responding to the text

Write your answers for each question in full sentences. Then discuss your answers with a partner.

1. Prapulla is going to live in New York with her new husband. How does her husband want her to dress? Why do you think so? _____

   _____

   _____

2. What do you think Prapulla will wear in New York? Why do you think so?

   _____

   _____

   _____

3. Why is Prapulla's wedding sari important to her? _____

   _____

   _____

   _____

Freewriting

Write for ten minutes on the topic below. Express yourself as well as you can. Don't worry about mistakes.

Prapulla has special memories and feelings about her wedding sari. On a separate piece of paper, write about a piece of clothing that is special to you.
- What does it look like?
- How did you get it?
- Why is it important to you?
- How does it make you feel?

In Part 2 you will ...
• learn about descriptive organization.
• brainstorm ideas and specific vocabulary to use in your writing.
• create an outline for your descriptive paragraph.

PART 2

Brainstorming and Outlining

✏️ WRITING TASK

In this unit, you will write a descriptive paragraph about a special possession.

Exercise 1 Brainstorming ideas

A. Review your freewriting exercise. Write the piece of clothing you freewrote about in the chart below. Then think of some other items you own that have a special meaning for you. Add them to the chart as well.

Jewelry	Photographs	Mechanical or electronic devices	Art or music	Clothing

B. Circle two or three items that you might like to write about. Describe these items to a partner.

Exercise 2 Brainstorming vocabulary

A. With a partner, think of words that you could use to describe items in the categories below. A few descriptive words have already been added to the chart.

Jewelry	Photographs	Mechanical or electronic devices	Art or music	Clothing
silver delicate round	faded serious happy	useful convenient practical	cheerful dramatic	colorful worn silk

B. Select some descriptive words from the chart on page 33 and use them to write five sentences about the items you circled.

My grandmother's gold watch is delicate.

_____

_____

_____

_____

Rhetorical Focus

Descriptive Organization

A descriptive paragraph describes a person, place, or thing so that the reader can picture it in his or her mind.

Topic Sentence
- The topic sentence in a descriptive paragraph introduces the item that the writer will describe.
- It may also include the writer's general feeling or opinion about the item.

Supporting Sentences
- The supporting sentences give some background information about the item.
- The supporting sentences also give descriptive details about the item. These details describe how the item looks, smells, feels, or tastes.
- The supporting sentences may also describe in more detail how the writer feels about the item.

Concluding Sentence
- The paragraph ends with a concluding sentence that restates the idea in the topic sentence using different words.

Exercise 3   **Reading a student paragraph**

Read the paragraph. What does the writer plan to do with the car?

The Long Life of my Grandfather's Car

I own a car that has special meaning for me because it belonged to my grandfather. When he was a young man, he saved money so he could buy a beautiful car to use on trips around the country. He finally bought a Cadillac convertible. It was white and blue with silver trim. There were white circles on the tires, and it had a powerful horn that made people jump out of his way. The seats were also white, but the dashboard was black. The steering wheel had a brown leather cover. The mats were gray and always clean. My grandfather took very good care of the car, and after he died my uncle gave it to me. I am very happy because it still has the original motor, and the body is intact. If it has problems, I will fix it myself. I plan to take very good care of my grandfather's car because someday I will use it to travel to all the states and cities that my grandfather visited when he was a young man.

Exercise 4 — Examining the student paragraph

A. Respond to the paragraph by answering the questions below.

1. Which of the following sentences best describes the main idea of the paragraph?
   a. The writer's grandfather traveled around the country in the 1950's.
   b. The writer likes Cadillac convertibles.
   c. The writer has strong feelings about his grandfather's Cadillac convertible.

2. Which of the following types of details did the author NOT include in the paragraph?
   a. appearance
   b. smell
   c. sound

3. According to the last sentence, why is the car important to the author?
   a. It connects the writer to his grandfather.
   b. The writer likes expensive cars.
   c. The writer likes to work on cars and repair engines.

B. Examine the organization of the paragraph by answering the questions below. Then compare your answers with a partner.

1. Underline the topic sentence in the paragraph.

2. What words or phrases does the author use to describe his grandfather's car?

_____

_____

3. What words or phrases does the author use to describe his feelings about the car?

_____

_____

4. Underline the concluding sentence twice.

Exercise 5 **Completing an outline**

Look back at the paragraph on page 35. Then fill in the missing information in the outline below.

Topic Sentence

Item the author describes: _____

The author's general feeling about the item: _____

_____

_____

Supporting Sentences

Background information about the item: _____

_____

_____

Descriptive details about the item: _____

_____

_____

Details about the author's feelings: _____

_____

_____

Concluding Sentence

Restated idea: _____

_____

Writing an outline

Review your brainstorming ideas and your freewriting exercise. Then use the chart below to write an outline for your paragraph about a special possession you own. Use the outline on page 36 as an example.

Topic Sentence

What are you going to describe? _____

_____

What is your general feeling about the possession? _____

_____

_____

Supporting Sentences

Write some notes about the background or history of the possession. _____

_____

_____

What are some details you can use to describe the possession? _____

_____

_____

What are some details you can use to describe your feelings about the

possession? _____

_____

_____

Concluding Sentence

Restate the idea in the topic sentence. _____

_____

_____

In Part 3 you will ...

- learn to use specific language in your writing.
- write a first draft of your descriptive paragraph.

PART 3

Developing Your Ideas

Exercise 1   **Reading a student paragraph**

Read the paragraph. How does the "treasure" make the author feel?

My Special Treasure

My special treasure is a picture of my mother on her fifteenth birthday. This picture was always in my house when I was growing up. Years later, when I got married and moved to Montreal, my mother gave it to me so that I would always remember her. Now it sits on the table next to my bed. I look at it and imagine my mother's life on that day. I think she was excited because her eyes are shining with happiness. Her smile is shy as if she were thinking about a secret. She is standing next to a rose bush, and the roses are taller than she is. She is wearing a beautiful white lace dress and black shoes. Her hair is long and curly. She looks lovely in this peaceful place, and I feel calm when I gaze into her eyes at the end of my busy day. This picture of my mother is my most valuable possession.

Exercise 2   **Examining the student paragraph**

A. Respond to the paragraph by answering the questions below in full sentences.

1. What is the author's special treasure? _____

   _____

   _____

2. Why does the author like this possession? _____

   _____

   _____

3. Who gave it to the author? _____

   _____

   _____

4. What words does the author use to describe the possession? _____

_____

_____

B. Examine the organization of the paragraph by answering the questions below. Then compare your answers with a partner.

1. Underline the topic sentence. What will the writer describe? _____

_____

2. Does the writer give details about how she got the picture in the first part, the middle part, or the last part of the paragraph? _____

_____

3. Does the writer describe what the picture looks like in the first part, the middle part, or the last part of the paragraph? _____

_____

4. Does the writer describe her thoughts and feelings about the picture in the first part, the middle part, or the last part of the paragraph? _____

_____

5. Underline the concluding sentence twice. Does it restate the idea in the topic sentence? _____

6. How many sentences are there in the paragraph? _____

Language Focus

Using Specific Language

Using specific language in descriptive writing helps give the reader a clear mental image of what something looks, feels, sounds, or smells like. Read the following examples. Which set of sentences has a stronger effect?

General Sentences	Sentences with Specific Language
He bought a vehicle.	He bought a 1965 Cadillac.
We heard a noise.	We heard the sound of breaking glass.
Suddenly, I smelled food.	Suddenly, I smelled steak and onions.

In the first column, the words are general and could be used to describe a variety of vehicles, noises, or food. In the second column, the writer has replaced the general terms with more specific words for the topics being described. By doing this, the writer has made the topic specific and clearer for the reader.

Identifying Specific Language

> **Read the following pairs of sentences. Put a check (✓) next to the sentence that is more specific.**

1. _____ a. I like to wear my grandmother's jewelry.

   __✓__ b. I like to wear my grandmother's pearl necklace.

2. _____ a. My best friend gave me a novel by Chang-Rae Lee for my birthday.

   _____ b. My best friend gave me a book for my birthday.

3. _____ a. Someone lent her an umbrella.

   _____ b. Her father lent her an umbrella.

4. _____ a. I inherited some furniture.

   _____ b. I inherited my grandmother's chair.

5. _____ a. Steve has a new laptop.

   _____ b. Steve has a new computer.

6. _____ a. Jordan received a toy.

   _____ b. Jordan received a teddy bear.

Adding specific details

> **Rewrite the following sentences. Replace the underlined words and phrases with words that are more specific.**

1. I bought <u>a pair of shoes</u>.

   I bought a pair of running shoes.
   _____

2. Maria found <u>some jewelry</u> in the basement.

   _____

3. My mother gave me <u>some money</u>.

   _____

4. I like <u>my desk</u>.

   _____

5. My father enjoyed making <u>things</u>.

   _____

6. My grandparents collected <u>souvenirs</u>.

   _____

7. We always have <u>vegetables</u> with dinner.

   _____

Editing a paragraph for specific language

A. **Read the following paragraph. Underline five words or phrases that could be more specific. Then for each underlined word or phrase, write one question below that you could ask the writer to help him or her be more specific.**

My Lost Treasure Box

When I left <u>my home town</u>, my relative gave me a special box. She said I could use the box to keep my special treasures. The box was made of a special material, and it was painted a bright color. When I opened it, it played a pretty song. I kept this box on my dresser and I used it to store my things. Unfortunately, I lost my beautiful box when I moved to a different city, but I will always remember it and my relative who gave it to me.

---

1. <u>What town did you come from?</u>

2. _____

3. _____

4. _____

5. _____

6. _____

B. **Rewrite the paragraph on a separate piece of paper, changing the underlined words and phrases to make them more specific. When you finish, compare your paragraph with a partner's.**

Writing a first draft

Review your outline. Then write your first draft of a paragraph about a possession that is important to you.

Peer editing a first draft

After you write your first draft, exchange it with a partner. Answer the questions on the checklist on page 42. You may also write comments or questions on your partner's draft. Then read your partner's comments on your draft, and revise it as necessary.

Editor's Checklist

Put a check (✓) as appropriate. Write answers in complete sentences in the lines provided.

☐ 1. Does the paragraph have a topic sentence? Can you identify the possession the writer will describe?

☐ 2. Does the writer provide background information about the possession? If so, write it here. _____

_____

_____

☐ 3. Does the paragraph have enough descriptive details to make the description clear to the reader?

☐ 4. Does the writer use specific words (instead of general terms) in the description? If there are words that could be more specific, write them here. _____

_____

☐ 5. Does the paragraph have a concluding sentence that restates the idea in the topic sentence?

In Part 4 you will ...

- learn to use adjectives in descriptive writing.
- learn to use the verb *be* to describe and define.
- edit your first draft for mistakes.

Editing Your Writing

Now that you have written a first draft, it is time to edit. Editing involves making changes to your writing to improve it and correct mistakes.

Language Focus

Using Adjectives in Descriptive Writing

Adjectives are words that describe nouns. Writers use adjectives to give the reader a more complete picture of the people, places, and things they want to describe. Compare the following pairs of phrases. Notice how the adjectives help you visualize the object.

a bicycle ⟶ a **racing** bicycle.
a desk ⟶ a **large**, **metal** desk.

- An adjective can come before a noun. If the noun is singular, use *a/an* or *the* before the adjective.

  I own **an antique** violin.
  My mother gave me **a big** hug.

- Adjectives have only one form. Use the same adjective with singular and plural nouns.

  a **lovely** bracelet
  two **lovely** bracelets

- An adjective can come after *be*. When two adjectives come after *be*, separate them with *and*.

  These shoes are **comfortable**.
  My father's expression is **wise and serious**.

- Nouns can also function as adjectives. In the following examples, the first noun describes the second noun.

  a **rose** garden
  a **pocket** knife

⚠ When a noun functions as an adjective, it is always singular.

  two **kitchen** tables
  two kitchens tables (INCORRECT)

Identifying adjectives

Read the following sentences and underline the adjectives.

1. I take care of my <u>sturdy</u>, <u>old</u> bicycle.

2. I am fond of my house plant.

3. It has broad green leaves and delicate, white flowers.

4. I bought a straw hat at a music festival.

5. It was not expensive, but I liked it because it was practical and attractive.

6. I bought my mug at a small tourist shop at the Phoenix airport.

Using adjectives

Change the following sentences by adding two or three adjectives to each one.

1. My umbrella is like a friend.

   <u>My big, black umbrella is like an old friend.</u>

2. I love my bicycle.

   _____

3. No one understands why I still wear my jeans.

   _____

4. If I could only save one thing from a fire, it would be my chair.

   _____

5. The piano in my parents' house is located in the room.

   _____

6. My mother gave me her ring.

   _____

Language Focus

Using *Be* to Describe and Define

Use the verb *be* to describe the subject of a sentence. You can use either a noun or an adjective after *be*.

• You can use *be* + adjective to describe conditions, physical characteristics, age, and personality.

Condition	Physical Characteristic	Age	Personality
He **is** <u>ready</u>.	I **am** <u>strong</u>.	My daughter **is** <u>six</u>.	Gabriela **is** <u>gracious</u>.

- You can use *be* + noun (or noun phrase) to identify or define something, or to describe occupations and relationships.

Identifying	**Describing Occupations**	**Describing Relationships**
It **is** <u>a map</u>.	He **is** <u>a waiter</u>.	We **are** <u>classmates</u>.

⚠ In academic writing the contracted forms of the verb *be* are not acceptable. Use the full forms of the verb in both affirmative and negative sentences.

The marmoset **is** a small mammal.
They **are** not responsible for the research.

Be with Adjectives		
SUBJECT	*BE*	ADJECTIVE
I	am am not	healthy.
He She	is is not	athletic.
You We They	are are not	young.

Be with Nouns		
SUBJECT	*BE*	NOUN PHRASE
I	am am not	an honest person.
He She	is is not	a dancer.
You We They	are are not	brothers.

Exercise 3   **Using *be* with adjectives**

Finish the following sentences with a form of the verb *be* and one or more adjectives to describe people you know.

1. My teacher <u>is creative</u>.

2. My classmates _____.

3. My parents _____.

4. My neighbors _____.

5. My cousins and I _____.

6. I _____.

Exercise 4   **Using *be* with nouns**

Finish each sentence below. Make sure there is a noun in your answer.

1. There is <u>an inhaler</u> for my asthma in my backpack.

2. There is _____ on my desk.

3. My father is _____.

4. Someone who writes novels is _____.

5. There is _____ downtown.

6. Someone who designs houses is _____.

Exercise 5   Editing a paragraph

Read the paragraph. Correct the mistakes with adjectives. There are five mistakes. For help review the rules on page 43.

> I have a new digital camera, and I am very excited about using it because it has so many features useful. I do not need to spend a lot of time focusing it. It has automatic focus. People do not have to wait a long time for me to take their picture. In addition, its lens is powerful. I can photograph a person and scenery, and both are clear when I print the finals pictures. Another feature allows me to delete pictures blurry. I save a lot of money because I do not have to print ugly pictures. I am very excited about my new camera because it is convenient easy, and I can take interestings pictures with it. I expect to have a lot of fun with it.

Exercise 6   Editing your first draft and rewriting

Review your paragraph for mistakes. Use the checklist below. Then write a final draft.

Editor's Checklist

Put a check (✓) as appropriate.

☐ 1. Did you include adjectives in your sentences to give your reader a more complete picture?

☐ 2. Did you use adjectives after articles and before nouns?

☐ 3. Did you use the verb *be* before adjectives and nouns?

☐ 4. Did you capitalize the first letter of each sentence and put end punctuation at the end?

In Part 5 you will ...

- review the elements of a descriptive paragraph.
- review adjectives and the verb *be*.
- practice writing with a time limit.

Putting It All Together

In this part of the unit, you will complete four exercises to improve your accuracy, write a timed paragraph to improve your fluency, and explore topics for future writing.

Exercise 1 **Using specific language**

Rewrite the following sentences. Replace the underlined words and phrases with words that are more specific.

1. I am reading a book.

   _____

2. In the photograph, the person is holding something.

   _____

3. Laura went to Europe for a while.

   _____

4. It is a picture of a monument.

   _____

5. The water flows through a forest.

   _____

6. Our room looked out over some scenery.

   _____

Exercise 2 **Identifying adjectives**

Read the following sentences. Underline the adjectives.

1. We planted a vegetable garden behind the house.

2. Friendly people are usually happy.

3. She has a different idea.

4. My favorite books are historical novels.

5. The class is upset about the math test.

Using adjectives

Rewrite the following sentences and add two or three adjectives to each one.

1. My brother owned a car.

   _____

2. My friend has a sister.

   _____

3. The man was a teacher.

   _____

4. This object is actually a computer.

   _____

5. I have a plant and a cat.

   _____

6. There is a tree next to the house.

   _____

Editing a paragraph

Read the paragraph. Correct the mistakes with adjectives. There are six mistakes.

> My most valuable possession is a handmade Persian carpet. My parents gave it to me as wedding gift right before I married my husband. This carpet is made of wool and silk. It is rectangular in shape, and it has a gold fringe along the borders. The colors of my carpet are mostly dark red on a cream colored background, but there are also blue and browns designs woven into it. In the center of the carpet, a round medallion is decorated with exquisites lines and curves. The carpet is not thick soft, but it is lovely to look at. I keep it in my living room because it reminds me of my parents wonderful, and the country beautiful where it was made.

 TIMED WRITING: 45 minutes

Write a descriptive paragraph about your favorite place to visit. Before you begin to write, review the following time management strategy.

BRAINSTORMING: 5 minutes

Write down some interesting places you have visited. Then write down some specific details about each place. When you finish, choose the place you would like to write a descriptive paragraph about.

Step 2 **OUTLINING: 5 minutes**

Write an outline for your paragraph.

Topic Sentence

Topic: _____

_____

General feeling about the topic: _____

_____

Supporting Sentences

Background information: _____

_____

_____

Details that describe the topic: _____

_____

_____

Details that describe how you feel about the topic: _____

_____

_____

Concluding Sentence

_____

_____

Step 3 **WRITING: 25 minutes**

Use your brainstorming notes and outline to write your first draft on a separate piece of paper.

When you have finished your first draft, check it for mistakes, using the checklist below.

Editor's Checklist

Put a check (✓) as appropriate.

☐ 1. Does the paragraph have a topic sentence that introduces the thing you will describe?

☐ 2. Did you include background information about the thing you are describing?

☐ 3. Did you include descriptive details about how the thing looks, smells, tastes, sounds, feels, etc?

☐ 4. Did you use specific words as part of your description?

☐ 5. Did you use adjectives as part of your description?

☐ 6. Are adjectives used correctly? (Refer to the rules on p. 43)

☐ 7. Does the paragraph have a concluding sentence that restates the idea in the topic sentence?

Topics for Future Writing

1. **Write a descriptive paragraph on one of the following topics.**

   - A person that you admire (outside of your family)
   - A favorite piece of art or music
   - Your favorite room in your home
   - A way to travel that interests you (by bicycle, train, hot air balloon)

2. **Interview a friend, classmate, or relative about his or her views on one of the topics above. Take notes during the interview. Then write a descriptive paragraph on the topic, but from your friend's point of view.**

Unit 3

Example Paragraphs

Unit Goals

Rhetorical Focus
- example organization
- using examples as supporting details

Language Focus:
- forming and using the simple present
- subject-verb agreement

PART 1

Stimulating Ideas

Writers use examples to help readers understand what they mean. A good example supports a more general idea with something specific. In this unit, you will write a paragraph that uses examples as supporting details.

Exercise 1 **Thinking about the topic**

Discuss the picture with a partner.

- Who is the little girl with?
- Who do you think she is talking to?
- Where do you think she might be going?
- What do you think her daily activities might be?
- Would you describe her life as "busy?" Why or why not?

Exercise 2 **Reading about the topic**

Three-year-old Olivia lives in busy New York City and has an imaginary friend. What is the main problem with this imaginary friend?

Bumping Into Mr. Ravioli

My daughter Olivia, who just turned three, has an **imaginary** friend whose name is Charlie Ravioli. Olivia is growing up in Manhattan, and so Charlie Ravioli has a lot of local **traits**: he lives in an apartment "on Madison and Lexington;" he **dines on** grilled chicken, fruit, and bottled water; and, having reached the age of seven and a half, he feels, or is thought, "old." But the most peculiarly local thing about Olivia's imaginary **playmate** is this: he is always too busy to play with her. She holds her toy cell phone up to her ear, and we hear her talk into it: "Ravioli? It's Olivia … It's Olivia. Come and play? O.K. Call me. Bye." Then she **snaps** it shut, and shakes her head. "I always get his machine," she says. Or she will say, "I spoke to Ravioli today." "Did you have fun?" my wife and I ask. "No. He was busy working. On a television" (leaving it up in the air if he repairs electronic devices or has his own talk show).

Gopnik, A. "Bumping into Mr. Ravioli." *The New Yorker:* September 30, 2002.

imaginary: existing only in the imagination
traits: features, characteristics
dines on: eats

playmate: a child's companion in play or recreation
snap: close with a sharp sound

Exercise 3   Understanding the text

Write *T* for true or *F* for false for each statement.

_____ 1. Olivia is three years old.

_____ 2. Charlie Ravioli is a real person.

_____ 3. Olivia often plays with Charlie Ravioli.

_____ 4. Charlie Ravioli is very different from most New Yorkers.

_____ 5. Olivia often talks to Charlie Ravioli in person.

Exercise 4   Responding to the text

Write your answers for each question in full sentences. Then discuss your answers with a partner.

1. Who is Olivia? _____

_____

2. Who is Charlie Ravioli? _____

_____

3. According to the author, is Charlie Ravioli a typical New Yorker? Why do you

think so? _____

_____

_____

4. What does Charlie Ravioli eat and drink? Why do you think the author

includes these details? _____

_____

_____

Exercise 5 **Freewriting**

**Write for ten minutes on the topic below. Express yourself as well as
you can. Don't worry about making mistakes.**

The writer describes Charlie Ravioli as a busy person. How would you describe
yourself? On a separate piece of paper, make a list of four or five adjectives that you
would use to describe yourself. Then write about why each one describes you. You
may choose from the list below or use other adjectives.

active	athletic	boring	busy
compassionate	confident	courageous	creative
difficult	flexible	fun	generous
hardworking	healthy	intelligent	organized
proud	shy	stubborn	

In Part 2 you will …

- learn about example organization.
- brainstorm ideas and specific vocabulary to use in
  your writing.
- create an outline for your example paragraph.

PART 2

Brainstorming and Outlining

✎ WRITING TASK

In this unit, you will write an example paragraph that describes you and your life. You will use specific examples to support your ideas.

Exercise 1 Brainstorming ideas

A. Review your freewriting exercise. Then choose one adjective from your freewriting exercise that you would like to write about. Use that adjective to complete the sentence below. This will be your topic sentence.

I am a/an _____ person.

B. Complete questions 1 and 2 below with the same adjective. Then write your answers to the questions.

1. What experiences have you had that show you are a/an _____ person?

   _____

   _____

   _____

2. What activities do you often do that show you are a/an _____ person?

   _____

   _____

   _____

Exercise 2 Brainstorming vocabulary

A. Read the following lists of adjectives. Add any new words you can think of to the chart. Use your dictionary for help.

Personality	cheerful, outgoing, optimistic, adventurous, _____
Feelings	peaceful, nervous, embarrassed, gloomy, excited, _____
Appearance	stocky, petite, graceful, handsome, _____
Characteristics	intelligent, creative, social, organized, athletic, _____

B. Choose four words from the chart that you might use as examples in your paragraph. Write a practice sentence with each word you choose.

1. _I am shy. For example, I feel nervous when I meet new people._

2. _____

3. _____

4. _____

5. _____

Rhetorical Focus

Example Organization

An example paragraph gives examples so that the reader clearly understands the writer's ideas about a topic.

Topic Sentence
- The first sentence introduces the topic.
- It also includes the controlling idea, or what the writer will say about the topic.

Supporting Sentences
- The middle sentences give examples that support the controlling idea.
- These examples give a clear picture of the writer's specific meaning.

Concluding Sentence
- The last sentence of the paragraph restates the topic and what the writer has said about it.

| Exercise 3 | **Reading a student paragraph** |

Read the student paragraph. Why is the title "Like a Mule"? Who in the paragraph is like a mule?

Like a Mule

I am a stubborn person. My friends and relatives are sure about this because they have experience with me. For example, I do not take advice from other people. When I was looking for work, I had to make a choice between two jobs. My mother and my husband wanted me to take a job in a childcare center, but I did not like it. I was stubborn, and I did not take their advice. I took a different job at a bookstore. Also, I do not change my mind easily. For example, when I bought my car, I wanted it in white. The car dealer had all the other colors, green, gold, blue, even red. I said no, and we went to a different dealer on the freeway about 50 miles away. They had the car in white. Now I am driving a white car. Also, I always defend my opinions. For example, I do not like the wife of my husband's friend. She is a mean person, and I told her what I thought of her, so we do not spend time together as couples. My life is not always easy, but I am proud to be a strong and stubborn woman.

Exercise 4 **Analyzing the student paragraph**

A. **Respond to the paragraph by answering the questions below in full sentences.**

1. What are the three main ways in which the author is stubborn? _____

_____

_____

_____

2. Why does the author say her life is not easy? _____

_____

_____

_____

B. **Examine the organization of the paragraph by answering the questions below. Then compare answers with a partner.**

1. Circle the topic and underline the controlling idea.

2. Read the second sentence. What do you expect the supporting details to describe? _____

3. How many examples does the author give? _____

4. Write one example that shows the author's stubbornness. _____

_____

5. Do all the supporting sentences support the topic sentence? _____

6. Underline the concluding sentence twice. Does it restate the topic sentence?

   _____

7. What does the author add to the concluding sentence that is not in the topic sentence? _____

   _____

8. In your opinion, does the author like being stubborn? Explain your answer.

   _____

   _____

Exercise 5   **Writing an outline**

Review your brainstorming ideas and your freewriting exercise. Then use the form to write an outline for your example paragraph. You do not need to write in full sentences. Use only the words that are necessary for remembering the information you want to include in your paragraph.

Topic Sentence

   I am a/an _____ person.

Supporting Sentences

   Example 1: _____

   _____

   _____

   Example 2: _____

   _____

   _____

   Example 3: _____

   _____

   _____

Concluding Sentence

   Restate the idea in the topic sentence. _____

   _____

   _____

In Part 3 you will ...

• learn more about using examples as supporting details.
• write a first draft of your example paragraph.

Reading a student paragraph

Read this student paragraph. What is the game the author refers to in the title?

My Game

I am an athletic guy. I like to watch sports on television, but I love playing sports even more. My favorite sport is soccer because it requires team work. I enjoy working with other players as a team. I am in two leagues. On both teams, I play forward because I am aggressive and can score goals. One of the leagues is just for fun, so I can mess around with my cousins and friends. The other league is more serious. I have to keep myself in good condition. There are regular practices and we work on special plays. Sometimes we travel to other cities in the state. I am also a student, so it is difficult to work around my school schedule. Basketball is another one of my sports. I often play at the park with my friends. Basketball is fun even though I am not so skillful. My friends and I joke while we play and have a good time. I also like swimming, but I do not swim in competitions. Mainly I swim to stay in shape for soccer. Playing sports is the thing that I enjoy most, and I especially like soccer because I feel happy when my team and I play well together.

Analyzing the student paragraph

A. Respond to the paragraph by answering the questions below in full sentences.

1. What is the author's favorite sport? What do you learn about him as a player?

   _____

   _____

2. Why does the author like soccer? _____

_____

_____

3. What other sports does the author participate in? _____

_____

_____

4. What examples does the author give that show how the two soccer leagues
are different? _____

_____

_____

5. Are you convinced that the author is athletic? Explain. _____

_____

_____

**B. Examine the organization of the paragraph by answering the
questions below. Then compare your answers with a partner.**

1. Circle the topic and underline the controlling idea in the topic sentence.

2. Read the second sentence. What do you expect the supporting details to
describe? _____

_____

3. Write one example that shows the author is athletic. _____

_____

4. Do all the details support the topic sentence? _____

5. Underline the concluding sentence. Does it restate the topic? _____

6. What does the author add to the concluding sentence that is not in the topic
sentence? _____

_____

Rhetorical Focus

Using Examples as Supporting Details

Effective examples have the following features:

- They are specific.
- They relate clearly to the controlling idea.
- They do not simply restate the topic sentence.

Read the following topic sentence:

| topic | controlling idea |

My mother is a good neighbor.

Now read the following supporting sentences. They both support the controlling idea by giving concrete, specific examples.

She always invites people from our neighborhood over for dinner.

Every year she hosts a back-to-school party for the children on our block.

Now read these sentences, which are not effective examples.

She enjoys gardening. *(not clearly related to the controlling idea)*
She is a wonderful person to live around. *(restates the controlling idea)*

An example often begins with the phrase *For example*, or *For instance*, followed by a comma.

He likes to stay in shape. **For example**, he runs six miles every day before work.

Sometimes writers use a semi colon to connect a general sentence with a specific example beginning with *for example*, or *for instance*.

Our teacher is entertaining; **for instance**, sometimes he uses puppets to teach grammar.

Exercise 3   **Identifying specific examples**

Read the following topic sentences. Then put a check next to the examples that support the topic sentence in the most specific way.

1. To become a good writer, a student should write often.

   _____ a. For example, she should try to write every day because writing is important.

   _✓_ b. For example, she should keep a journal and write in it every evening before bed.

   _✓_ c. For example, she can find an email friend and write messages frequently.

2. Living in the city is challenging in many ways.

   _____ a. City dwellers usually pay a lot of money to live in a small apartment.

   _____ b. It is difficult to live in a city because of the lifestyle in cities.

   _____ c. People who live in the city have to deal with pollution.

3. My sister is easy to tease.

     ____ a. For instance, many people like to joke with her.

     ____ b. For instance, I often tell her that I am getting married, and she always believes me.

     ____ c. For instance, she has a cheerful personality and she does not get angry when I make jokes about her boyfriends.

4. This school offers a lot of opportunities to students.

     ____ a. There are many clubs and organizations students can join.

     ____ b. The school tries to help students.

     ____ c. The school has a career counseling center that offers advice and workshops for students.

5. The world is becoming smaller.

     ____ a. For instance, it is easy to see that many things are changing in the world.

     ____ b. For instance, new forms of communication make it easy for people from different countries to work together on projects.

     ____ c. For instance, many Asian people can spend part of the year in the U.S. and part of the year in Asia because it is easy to travel back and forth.

Exercise 4 Making examples specific

Read the passages below. Underline the example. Then revise each example to make it more specific.

1. I have a very patient cat. <u>For instance, she never gives up.</u>
   <u>For instance, she can sit in front of a mouse hole for hours.</u>

2. My doctor is a caring person. For example, he is very nice to patients.

   _____

3. The neighbors in my apartment building are noisy. For example, I can't sleep at night because they are making a lot of noise.

   _____

4. My friend has a great sense of humor. For example, she always makes me laugh.

   _____

5. My nephew is naughty. For instance, he is always getting into trouble.

   _____

6. My friend is very talented. For example, she can do many things.

   _____

Writing specific examples

Write two examples as supporting details for each of the following topic sentences. Make sure the examples are specific.

1. My friend loves animals.

   She always brings homeless animals to the pet shelter.

   She takes care of several animals in her home.

2. I am a busy person.

   _____

   _____

3. There are many things to see in my city.

   _____

   _____

4. Cell phones are useful for many different situations.

   _____

   _____

5. My sister is beautiful.

   _____

   _____

6. My neighbors are generous.

   _____

   _____

Writing a first draft

Review your outline. Then write the first draft of an example paragraph about yourself.

Peer editing a first draft

After you write your first draft, exchange it with a partner. Answer the questions on the checklist on page 64. You may also write comments or questions on your partner's draft. Then read your partner's comments on your first draft, and revise it as necessary.

Editor's Checklist

Put a check (✓) as appropriate. Write answers in the lines provided.

☐ 1. Does the paragraph have a title? Write the title here. If there is no title, suggest a title. _____

_____

☐ 2. Does the paragraph have a topic sentence that introduces the topic and has a controlling idea? If the topic sentence does not have a controlling idea, suggest a controlling idea.

_____

_____

☐ 3. Do the supporting details give examples that support the topic sentence? Write the examples here. _____

_____

_____

☐ 4. Are all the supporting examples relevant? Write down any that seem unrelated to the topic. _____

_____

_____

☐ 5. Does the concluding sentence restate the idea in the topic sentence?

☐ 6. Are you convinced that the main descriptive word that the writer uses as the controlling idea describes the writer well?

In Part 4 you will …

- learn about the simple present tense.
- learn about subject-verb agreement.
- edit your first draft for mistakes.

Editing Your Writing

Now that you have written a first draft, it is time to edit. Editing involves making changes to your writing to improve it and correct mistakes.

Language Focus

Using the Simple Present

Use the simple present tense to express habits and routines.

I wake up at 6:00 every day.

Also use the simple present to write about general truths and scientific facts.

Babies are a great responsibility.

The earth revolves around the sun.

Forming the Simple Present

Follow these rules to form the simple present tense:

- When the subject is first person (*I, we*), second person (*you*), or third person plural (*they, the boys*), use the base form of the verb.

- When the subject of a sentence is a third person singular pronoun (*he, she, it*), a singular name (*Martha, Los Angeles*), or a singular noun (*my friend, the boy*), add *–s* or *–es* to the base form of the verb.

- To form negative statements, use *do/does* + *not* + the base form of the verb.

  We **exercise** every day.   He **works** in Manhattan.   Elena **does not go** to school.

⚠ Speakers often contract *do not* and *does not* to *don't* and *doesn't*. However, contractions are not appropriate for written academic English.

Affirmative Statements		
SUBJECT	BASE FORM OF VERB OR BASE FORM OF VERB + -S/-ES	
I You	eat	healthy food.
He She It	eats	
We You They	eat	

Negative Statements			
SUBJECT	DO/DOES + NOT	BASE FORM OF VERB	
I You	do not	eat	healthy food.
He She It	does not		
We You They	do not		

Exercise 1 Practicing with the simple present

Complete these sentences with information about people you know. Use a present tense verb other than the verb *be*.

1. My father _reads a book every week._____

2. My cousin _____

3. Most of my classmates _____

4. My best friend _____

5. The children in my neighborhood_____

Language Focus

Subject-Verb Agreement

A verb must agree in number with its subject. Consider the examples. In the first sentence, a plural verb form (*are*) follows a plural pronoun (*we*). However, in the second sentence, a singular form (*is*) follows the plural subject (*we*). This sentence is incorrect.

We **are** tired.
We is tired. (INCORRECT)

Use a plural verb following two or more nouns that are joined by *and*.
Mary and her sister **live** in Las Vegas.

Use a singular verb following a group noun when it talks about the group as a whole.
The class **goes** on a field trip every month.

Use a singular verb following a noun in expressions that refer to a single member of a group.

One of the students **owns** a restaurant.
The leader of the wolves always **eats** first.

Practicing subject-verb agreement

Complete each sentence with the correct form of a present tense verb below.

cook/cooks	practice/practices	receive/receives
own/owns	do not work/does not work	

1. The team _____ at the stadium each morning.

2. One of my brothers _____ a brand new car.

3. Rachel and Julia _____ breakfast and dinner every day.

4. My sister and her boyfriend _____ on weekends.

5. Her fan club _____ at least 100 letters a week.

Editing a paragraph

Read the paragraph. Correct the mistakes with present tense verbs. There are ten mistakes.

My Talented Sisters

My sisters are both talented people. Vanessa and Rita is musicians. Vanessa is a piano player and Rita play the guitar. They are students at The High School for the Performing Arts. Vanessa and some other girls in her class is guest performers at churches and other events nearly every weekend. This are good practice for them because they wants to play professionally one day. My other sister, Rita, is younger than Vanessa. She is not ready to perform yet, but she play the guitar very well. She usually perform at family parties. They works hard. Every day when they comes home, they are tired, but sometimes they play music for us at home. We feels lucky to have such talented people in our family.

Review your paragraph for mistakes. Use the checklist below. Then write a final draft.

Editor's Checklist

Put a check (✓) as appropriate.

☐ 1. Did you check for subject-verb agreement?

☐ 2. Did you use present tense verbs correctly?

☐ 3. Did you check to make sure there are no contractions?

☐ 4. Did you capitalize the first letter of each sentence and put end punctuation at the end?

In Part 5 you will …

- review the elements of an example paragraph.
- write a timed example paragraph.

PART 5

Putting It All Together

In this part of the unit, you will complete five exercises to improve your accuracy, write a timed paragraph to improve your fluency, and then explore topics for future writing.

Exercise 1   Identifying examples as supporting details

Read the topic sentences and the examples that follow. Then put a check next to the examples that support the topic sentence.

1. Computers have made students' lives easier.

   _____ a. They can ask questions of their instructors by e-mail.

   _____ b. They can edit their papers easily by deleting their errors and typing new words or sentences.

   _____ c. They can form study groups and discuss topics in the library.

   _____ d. They can research information on the Internet.

2. Nabila is someone who is always ready to help.

   _____ a. For example, she enjoys going to parties.

   _____ b. For example, she is willing to lend her friends money if they ask for it.

   _____ c. For example, she takes time off to take care of a sick grandmother.

   _____ d. For example, she always asks if there is anything she can do for her friends.

3. Shopping online is more convenient than shopping at a department store.

   _____ a. You can shop online at any time of the day.

   _____ b. You can compare prices at several stores when shopping online.

   _____ c. You cannot touch the fabric of the clothes you order.

   _____ d. Since you do not have to leave your house, you will save on gas and time.

4. Reading is an important way to practice a new language.

   _____ a. For instance, reading improves vocabulary.

   _____ b. For instance, it is difficult to learn a new language.

   _____ c. For instance, reading helps people learn sentence patterns.

   _____ d. For instance, reading allows you to practice a new language.

5. The birth of my son helped me to become more patient.

_____ a. I exercised more to stay healthy for my son.

_____ b. I had to sit still for hours holding him in my arms until he fell sleep.

_____ c. Sometimes I had to spend up to two hours trying to feed him.

_____ d. When he was older, I went to movies with him.

Exercise 2   Writing specific examples

Write two examples as supporting details for each of the following topic sentences.

1. College students have a stressful life.

_____

_____

2. There are many advantages to being organized.

_____

_____

3. My high school years were the best time of my life.

_____

_____

4. My experiences with computers have been frustrating.

_____

_____

5. Taking a vacation on the beach is a lot of fun.

_____

_____

Exercise 3   Using the simple present

Complete the following sentences with information that includes a simple present tense verb.

1. Writing a good paragraph _____

2. Careful drivers _____

3. A tourist _____

4. My hometown _____

5. A hero _____

6. My cell phone _____

Practicing subject verb agreement

Complete each sentence with the correct form of a present tense verb below.

watches/watch	does not agree/do not agree	performs/perform
drives/drive	shares/share	studies/study

1. Harold and Ron _____ to work together at least twice a week.

2. My favorite band _____ at the state fair every year.

3. The president of the organization _____ with the committee's recommendation.

4. One of my sisters _____ too much television.

5. Canada and the United States _____ a border.

6. He _____ English and economics at the university.

Editing a paragraph

Read the paragraph. Correct the mistakes with present tense verbs. There are eight mistakes.

Trust

The most important quality of a friend is honesty. An honest friend never lie about anything. She tell you, for example, if she disagree with you on an issue. When you ask for advice, she tells you the truth even when it is difficult. When you asks an honest friend's opinion about the clothes you are wearing to a party, she tells you if they are inappropriate. If you does something bad, she do not hesitate to give you sincere feedback. This honesty result in trust between you and your friend. In short, honesty are the most important characteristic that I look for in a friend.

TIMED WRITING: 45 minutes

Write an example paragraph on the topic below. Before you begin to write, review the following time management strategy.

Describe your ideal English teacher. What is his or her most important characteristic?

Step 1 **BRAINSTORMING: 5 minutes**

What characteristics must a good English teacher have? Write down as many of these characteristics you can in the box or on a separate piece of paper. Then choose one characteristic that is the most important to you, and write four specific examples for the characteristic.

OUTLINING: 5 minutes

Write an outline for your paragraph.

Topic Sentence

_____

_____

Supporting Sentences

Example 1: _____

_____

_____

Example 2: _____

_____

_____

Example 3: _____

_____

_____

Example 4: _____

_____

_____

Concluding Sentence

_____

_____

WRITING: 25 minutes

Use your brainstorming notes and outline to write your first draft on a separate piece of paper.

When you have finished your first draft, check it for mistakes, using the checklist below. Make any changes necessary.

Editor's Checklist

Put a check (✓) as appropriate.

☐ 1. Does the topic sentence introduce the topic and contain a controlling idea?

☐ 2. Does the paragraph include specific examples to help the reader understand your point of view?

☐ 3. Do the examples support the topic and controlling idea?

☐ 4. Does the paragraph have a concluding sentence that restates the topic sentence?

☐ 5. Did you use present tense verbs correctly?

☐ 6. Do all the subjects and verbs agree?

☐ 7. Did you capitalize the first letter of each sentence and put end punctuation at the end?

Topics for Future Writing

1. Write an example paragraph on one of the following topics.

   - A good physician
   - Your favorite relative
   - A president/prime minister you would vote for
   - The worst waiter

2. Interview a friend, classmate, or relative about his or her views on one of the topics above. Take notes during the interview to use for your paragraph. Then write an example paragraph on one of the topics above, but from a friend's point view.

Process Paragraphs

Unit Goals

Rhetorical focus
- process organization

Language focus:
- using time order words in process paragraphs
- using imperatives
- modals of advice, necessity, and prohibition

PART 1

Stimulating Ideas

A process paragraph explains how to do something step by step. The reader should be able to follow the steps to get a desired result.

Exercise 1 | **Thinking about the topic**

Discuss the picture with a partner.

- What do you see in the picture?
- What is the person doing? Why?
- What do you think the person should do next? Why?
- Have you ever been frightened by another creature? Explain why and what happened.

Exercise 2 | **Reading about the topic**

Sharks sometimes attack swimmers or scuba divers in the ocean. What is the most important thing to do if a shark attacks you?

How to Fight Off a Shark

Most shark attacks occur near land, typically near or between **sandbars** where sharks feed. Attacks also happen in areas with steep **drop-offs**. Sharks gather in these areas because their natural **prey** is there. Almost any large shark, around six feet or longer in total length, is a danger to humans.

If a shark is coming toward you or attacks you, use anything you have in your possession to hit the shark's eyes or **gills**. These are the areas most sensitive to pain. Make quick, sharp, repeated **jabs** in these areas. Sharks are **predators** and will usually only follow through on an attack if they have the advantage, so making the shark unsure of its advantage in any way possible will increase your chances of survival. Contrary to popular opinion, the shark's nose is not the area to attack, unless you cannot reach the eyes or gills. Hitting the shark simply tells it that you are not **defenseless**.

If a shark shows itself to you, it might just be curious and may swim on and leave you alone. If you are under the surface and lucky enough to see an attacking shark then you do have a good chance of defending yourself if the shark is not too large.

sandbar: an underwater hill
drop-off: area of the ocean where the land falls away suddenly
prey: a person or animal that is hunted by another animal
gills: slits located in the sides of sharks that allow them to breath

jab: a fast blow, usually done with the fist
predator: A person or animal that hunts other living creatures for food
defenseless: unable to protect oneself

Exercise 3 | **Understanding the text**

Write *T* for true or *F* for false for each statement.

_____ 1. Sharks come close to land when they are hungry.

_____ 2. Sharks always attack people who are far away from the beach.

_____ 3. Most sharks will not attack humans.

_____ 4. If a shark attacks you, you should hit it in the nose.

_____ 5. If a shark sees you, it will probably attack you.

Responding to the text

Write your answers for each question in full sentences. Then discuss your answers with a partner.

1. You are swimming and you see a shark coming toward you. What should you do? _____

_____

_____

2. What should you not do? _____

_____

_____

3. When you are choosing a place to swim or scuba dive, what sort of places should you stay away from? _____

_____

_____

Freewriting

Write for ten minutes on the topic below. Express yourself as well as you can. Don't worry about making mistakes.

"How to Fight Off a Shark" explains the steps you should take to get out of a dangerous situation. Think of something that you know how to do that might be helpful to someone else. It does not have to be an emergency situation. It can be something simple such as packing a suitcase or changing the oil in a car. Consider the following questions as you write:

- What is the task?
- What will the result be?
- What do you need to do first? Second? Third?
- What should you avoid doing?

In Part 2 you will ...

- learn about process organization.
- brainstorm ideas and specific vocabulary to use in your writing.
- create an outline for your process paragraph.

PART 2

Brainstorming and Outlining

WRITING TASK

In this unit, you will write a process paragraph about something you know how to do that might be helpful to someone else.

Exercise 1 **Brainstorming ideas**

Review your freewriting exercise. Then do the following.

A. Think of some tasks and activities that you do often. Write them in the chart below. Then select one or two that are processes that require steps. Finally, put a check next to those activities that might be good topics for a process paragraph.

Time	Tasks and activitites
Morning	
Afternoon	
Evening	
Weekends	

B. Describe one of the tasks or activities in the chart to a partner.

A. Circle the words that you might like to use in your writing. Then add two or three words to each list.

Measure	a foot, a pound, a tablespoon, _____, _____, _____
Use	a knife, a hammer, a pencil, a pair of scissors, _____, _____, _____
Fill	a container, a bucket, a bottle, a bowl, _____, _____, _____
Insert	a screw, a wire, a hook, a tube, _____, _____, _____
Remove	dirt, shells, bones, twigs, the cap, the lid, _____, _____, _____

B. On a separate piece of paper, use vocabulary from the chart to write five sentences about your process.

Rhetorical Focus

Process Organization

A process paragraph describes the steps necessary to perform a process or task.

Topic Sentence
• The topic sentence introduces the process that the writer will explain.

Supporting Sentences
• The middle sentences describe a sequence of steps that give detailed information about the stages of the process.
• These sentences may also give background details that help define the process for the reader or explain why this process is useful or necessary.
• Supporting sentences may also include the tools needed for the task.

Concluding Sentence
- The paragraph ends with a concluding sentence that restates the topic sentence using different words.
- This sentence may also include a suggestion or warning to help the reader do the task more easily.

Exercise 3   **Reading a student paragraph**

Read the paragraph. What does the word "royalty" in the title refer to?

Royalty in your Garden

Roses are royalty among flowers. Many people say they are as difficult to maintain as kings and queens, but roses are actually quite easy to grow. All you need is a shovel and a few simple steps. In fact, growing roses can actually be fun. First, go to a nursery to purchase the rose plants. You will probably see many beautiful varieties, but it is best to choose only two or three rose bushes to start with. You should also purchase potting soil and rose food. After you bring your rose plants home, look for a sunny spot in your garden because roses love sunshine. Then dig a deep hole with a shovel and add a little potting soil and rose food. Next, transplant your roses from the pot to the garden. Cover the roots with more potting soil and then give your new roses a big drink of water. As long as they have sunshine and water, your roses will stay healthy all summer. When winter comes, your roses will lose their flowers and leaves and look dead. As a result, you might think about discarding them. Do not do that. Instead, this is the best time to prune them. Cut off the thin stems with garden shears so that the bush can become stronger the next spring. If you continue to take care of your roses in this simple way, they will produce beautiful flowers year after year.

A. Respond to the paragraph by answering the questions below in full sentences.

1. Why are some people afraid to grow rose plants? _____

_____

_____

2. What do roses need to be healthy? _____

_____

_____

3. What happens to rose plants in the winter? _____

_____

_____

4. Do you feel confident that you could raise roses after reading this paragraph? Why or why not? _____

_____

_____

B. Examine the organization of the paragraph by answering the questions below. Then compare your answers with a partner.

1. Underline the topic sentence. Which of the following statements best describes the main idea of the paragraph? (Check one.)

_____ a. Roses are very special flowers.

_____ b. Growing roses is easy.

_____ c. Roses are difficult to grow.

2. Which of the following types of details does the writer include in the paragraph? (Check all that apply.)

_____ a. the tools that are necessary for growing roses

_____ b. warnings about what not to do when growing roses

_____ c. steps that gardeners should take when growing roses

_____ d. the result of the task

3. Underline the concluding sentence twice. Which statement below best describes the concluding sentence? (Check one.)

_____ a. It is a warning about what can go wrong when growing roses.

_____ b. It tells the expected result of the process.

_____ c. It is a summary of the main steps.

Writing an outline

Review your brainstorming ideas and your freewriting exercise. Then use the chart below to write an outline for your process paragraph.

Topic Sentence

_____

_____

Supporting Sentences

Background information: _____

_____

_____

Step 1: _____

_____

Step 2: _____

_____

Step 3: _____

_____

Step 4: _____

_____

Step 5: _____

_____

Concluding Sentence

_____

_____

In Part 3 you will ...
• learn to use time order words in a process paragraph. • write a first draft of your process paragraph.

PART 3

Developing Your Ideas

Reading a student paragraph

Read the paragraph. What is the secret mentioned in the title?

The Secret to a Successful Vacation

Imagine that you are on vacation at the beach, and you open your suitcase to discover that you have forgotten your swimsuit! This and other disasters and inconveniences can be avoided if you follow certain steps when packing your suitcase. The first step is to review your travel plans and activities. Make a list and save it so that you can check your items before you leave. Next, gather the items you will need for your activities. Remove any item that is not necessary. Try to mix and match fewer pieces of clothing and shoes by choosing a color or colors that match. Third, you are ready to pack. Start with large items such as books or shoes. Stuff your shoes with extra socks to save space. Then place shoes in plastic bags and fit them into the corners of your suitcase. There should be plenty of room for the clothes. To avoid wrinkles, layer your clothes and roll them up. Put the rolls of clothing into the suitcase. Then put in the smaller items. Finally, before you close your suitcase, check your list. Make sure you have not forgotten your swimsuit! Many people like to swim while they are on vacation. It is worthwhile to take your time when you pack your suitcase because a well-packed suitcase is the secret to a good travel experience.

Analyzing the student paragraph

A. Respond to the paragraph by answering the questions below in full sentences.

1. Why is it important to review travel plans? _____

_____

_____

2. What is the author's strategy for packing only a few pieces of clothing?

_____

_____

3. What items does the author suggest putting in the suitcase first? Why?

_____

_____

4. What is the last step in packing a suitcase? _____

_____

_____

B. Examine the organization of the paragraph by answering the questions below. Then compare your answers with a partner.

1. Re-read the first two sentences. Which one is the topic sentence? Write it here.

_____

_____

2. Does the author give background information about why the process is important or useful? If so, what is the background information?

_____

_____

3. How many steps can you identify in the process? _____

4. What kinds of examples does the author provide to support the steps in the process?

_____

_____

5. Find one sentence that is unrelated to the topic and draw a line through it.

6. Underline the concluding sentence twice. Does it restate the topic sentence? Explain your answer.

_____

_____

Using Time Order Words in Process Paragraphs

Time order words tell the order of steps in a process. You can use *first* and *second* to indicate the first two steps in a process. Use *next, then, later,* or *after that* to add more steps. *Finally* marks the last step in the process.

First, make a list.

Second, select your clothes.

Next, place your shoes in the corners.

Then arrange your clothes in neat layers.

Later, add last minute items such as medications.

After that, roll the clothes to avoid wrinkles.

Finally, check your list for any forgotten items.

⚠ *Then* is not followed by a comma.

Connectors link two clauses together. Connectors like *before* and *after* can also function as time order words when they link two steps in a process.

Before you close your suitcase, check your list.

Begin packing **after** you have eliminated all unnecessary items.

Exercise 3   **Using time order words to identify the sequence of steps**

Number the steps in the following process according to how they should be followed. Use the time order words to help you decide the correct order.

It is easy to have a good dinner party if you follow some easy steps.

_____ a. Next, make a list of people that you would like to invite.

_____ b. After your house is clean, go shopping for food, flowers and decorations.

_____ c. Then make a funny or pretty invitation and email it to your friends.

_____ d. Finally, turn on the music, and wait for the fun to begin.

_____ e. Before the guests arrive, decorate the house, set the table, and take a shower.

_____ f. After you have everything you need, plan a meal and make sure you can cook most of it before your guests arrive.

_____ g. A few days before the party, start cleaning your house.

_____ h. First, choose an appropriate date at least two weeks before the party.

Practicing with time order words

Read the following paragraph. Fill in the blanks with appropriate time order words. Remember to use proper punctuation.

One big challenge that many people like is running in a marathon. A marathon is a race that is over 26 miles, so it is very hard to complete the race. If you want to run the entire course, you have to train diligently. _____ buy a good pair of comfortable
1.
running shoes. Then begin your running practice at least six months _____ you run in the race. Try to run three to six miles at
2.
least four times a week. You must also stretch before and after a run to avoid tight muscles. _____ your body is accustomed to longer
3.
runs, you can work on your strength by doing sprints, or short fast runs. _____ lengthen your runs to ten or 12 miles. Make sure
4.
you drink plenty of water when you go on longer runs because it is important for your muscles. When the day of the race is close, check your shoes. You might need a new pair. The night before you race, eat a lot of carbohydrates. They will give you energy for the big day. _____ on the day of the race, get up early and drink plenty of
5.
water. You should feel confident, strong, and ready to go.

Writing the steps in a process

Read the following topic. With a partner, write some important steps in the process. Use appropriate time order words.

Topic: How to buy a used car

Step 1: _____

_____

_____

Step 2: _____

_____

_____

Step 3: _____

_____

_____

Step 4: _____

_____

_____

Writing a first draft

Review your outline. Then write your first draft of a process paragraph about something you know how to do that might be helpful to someone else.

Peer editing a first draft

After you write your first draft, exchange it with a partner. Answer the questions on the checklist on page 89. You may also write comments or questions on your partner's draft. Then read your partner's comments on your first draft and revise it as necessary.

Editor's Checklist

Put a check (✓) as appropriate. Write answers in complete sentences in the lines provided.

☐ 1. Does the paragraph have a topic sentence? Can you identify the process the writer will describe?

☐ 2. Does the writer provide background information about the process? If so, write it here. _____

_____

☐ 3. Does the paragraph have time order words to help clarify the order of the steps in the process? If so, which time order words does the writer use? _____

_____

☐ 4. Does the writer explain why this process is useful or necessary and include the tools needed? If not, write the information that is missing here. _____

_____

☐ 5. Does the concluding sentence restate the main idea in the topic sentence or give a suggestion or warning?

In Part 4 you will ...

- learn about imperatives.
- learn to identify and use modals of advice, necessity, and prohibition.
- edit your first draft for mistakes.

Editing Your Writing

Now that you have written a first draft, it is time to edit. Editing involves making changes to your writing to improve it and correct mistakes.

Language Focus

Using Imperatives

Use imperative sentences to give instructions, directions, or to tell steps in a process.

- The verb in an imperative addresses the reader or listener directly.

- The imperative uses the base form of the verb.

- An imperative sentence does not require a subject, but the subject *you* is always implied.

  Hold the fishing rod gently in your right hand.

  Be quiet or you may disturb the fish.

For a negative imperative, use *do not*.

Do not let your finger get caught in the string.

Exercise 1 | **Identifying imperatives**

Put a check next to the imperative sentences.

___✓___ 1. Buy a good quality tape.

_____ 2. It is important to start early in the morning to avoid the heat.

_____ 3. Get down on your hands and knees and crawl under the smoke.

_____ 4. Try not to get chili powder in your eyes.

_____ 5. You should ask a professional to dispose of the used motor oil.

_____ 6. With your left hand, grab the red handle and pull it.

_____ 7. Getting out of a traffic jam is not too difficult if you follow this procedure.

Practicing with imperatives

Rewrite the following sentences as imperatives.

1. It is necessary to check the horse's back for sticks and insects before putting on the saddle blanket.

   Check the horse's back for sticks and insects before putting on the
   saddle blanket.

2. It is a good idea to fill water bottles and put them in the freezer the night before.

   _____

3. You should dress in comfortable clothing and sneakers or sandals.

   _____

4. It is important to debug your hard drive periodically.

   _____

5. You need to replace the water in the tank every week or two.

   _____

6. You must not leave the fire unattended.

   _____

Language Focus

Modals of Advice, Necessity, and Prohibition

Should and *must* are modal verbs. You can use modals to express advice, necessity, and prohibition. Modal verbs come before the base form of the verb.

   You **should eat** more vegetables   You **must arrive** by eight o'clock.

Advice

In a process paragraph, use the modal *should* to offer advice, tips, and suggestions for being more successful.

You **should** remove all jewelry before working with the clay.

Necessity

Use the modal *must* to explain rules and laws that affect a process or to explain something that is absolutely necessary.

You **must** wear protective headgear when you compete.

Use *do not have to* to say that something is not necessary.

You **do not have to** pay a fee to enter the museum.

Prohibition

In negative statements of prohibition, use *should* and *must* with *not* and the base form of the verb.

You **should not** open the oven while the cake is baking.
You **must not** drink alcohol.

Affirmative Statements with *Should* and *Must*

SUBJECT	SHOULD/MUST	BASE FORM OF VERB
I		
You		
He She It	should must	come.
We		
You		
They		

Negative Statements with *Should* and *Must*

SUBJECT	SHOULD/MUST + NOT	BASE FORM OF VERB
I		
You		
He She It	should not must not	come.
We		
You		
They		

Negative Statements with *Have to*

SUBJECT	DO/DOES + NOT	HAVE TO	BASE FORM OF VERB
I	do not		
You			
He She It	does not	have to	come.
We	do not		
You			
They			

Exercise 3 Using modals of advice, necessity, and prohibition

Complete each sentence with *should* or *must*. Then explain your choice of modal.

1. You ____should____ start early in the morning to avoid the traffic.

   This is advice, but it is not a necessity.

2. You _____ have a license to drive a car.

   _____

3. You _____ not bring guns into the airport.

_____

4. You look tired. You _____ get a good night's sleep.

_____

5. You _____ not leave a baby alone in a bathtub.

_____

Exercise 4 **Practicing with modal verbs**

**Use modal verbs to write one affirmative and one negative sentence
about each topic.**

1. Babysitting

   <u>You should ask about the child's bedtime.</u>

   <u>You must not leave the child alone outside.</u>

2. Changing a light bulb

   _____

   _____

3. Applying for a job

   _____

   _____

4. Taking a test

   _____

   _____

5. Driving in the rain

   _____

   _____

Exercise 5 **Editing a paragraph**

**Read the paragraph and correct any mistakes with imperatives or with
should or *must*. There are seven mistakes.**

People who are serious about managing their time better should
following this procedure. It will help you to have more control over
your time. First, you need to figure out how you actually spend your
time. You make a list of all the things you do daily. Writing down how
much time you spend on each thing. Include activities like talking on

the telephone or buying a cup of coffee. Your list will be quite long. Then find the activities that you can eliminate from your daily routine. It may be hard to give up a trip to the coffee shop, but you can do it. You must going to work, so you cannot eliminate that item, but you will probably find other items that are not necessary. You should dropped those unnecessary activities to make time for more important things. Next, prepare a schedule for yourself. Being realistic about the time of day you choose for certain activities. Make a schedule that you can follow. Not try to do too much. If you follow these steps and manage your schedule carefully, you will have a happier, more organized life.

Exercise 6   **Editing your first draft**

Review your paragraph for mistakes. Use the checklist below. Then write a final draft.

Editor's Checklist

Put a check (✓) as appropriate.

- ☐ 1. Did you use imperatives to give instructions or directions?
- ☐ 2. Did you use *should* to give tips and advice?
- ☐ 3. Did you use *must* to explain rules or necessities?
- ☐ 4. Did you use *not* with a modal to express prohibitions?
- ☐ 5. Did you use *do not have to* to explain that something is not necessary?
- ☐ 6. Did you capitalize the first letter of each sentence and put end punctuation at the end?

In Part 5 you will ...

- review the elements of a process paragraph.
- practice writing with a time limit.

Putting It All Together

In this part of the unit, you will complete three exercises to improve your accuracy, write a timed paragraph to improve your fluency, and then explore topics for future writing.

Exercise 1 Using time order words

Read the following paragraph. Fill in the blanks with appropriate time order words from the box. Use each word once. Remember to use proper punctuation.

then	second	finally	first	next

A bonsai is a small tree planted in a pot. It comes from the Japanese culture, but it is now a hobby of many people around the world. A bonsai is living art, and how it looks depends on your taste and skills. To create a bonsai, it is important to follow these steps. _____ 1. choose a tree that suits your interest and the location where it will be kept. Some trees do better inside the house and some look healthier outside. The tree must be young and big enough to resemble a mature tree. The size of the tree could be between 10 to 100 centimeters, depending on your taste. _____ 2. find a pot that is the right size for the tree. _____ 3. cut two-thirds off the roots of the tree in order to stop its natural growth. _____ 4. put the bonsai in the pot and add dirt fortified with minerals. _____ 5. give the bonsai a natural shape with special clippers. Creating a bonsai requires some time and patience, but it is certainly worth the effort.

Using imperatives

Rewrite the following sentences as imperatives.

1. You must buy a good fishing rod.

   _____

2. You should warn the patient before you give him an injection.

   _____

3. It is necessary to speak English with your classmates.

   _____

4. You need to type in your log-in ID and password.

   _____

5. You need to jog slowly at first.

   _____

Exercise 3 **Using *should* and *must***

Complete each sentence with *should* or *must*. Then explain your choice of modal.

1. You _____ not begin eating until the hostess does. It is not very polite.

   _____

2. You _____ arrive on time, or the boat will leave without you. Do not forget!

   _____

3. We _____ not wait until the last minute to pack.

   _____

4. You _____ drink plenty of water when you exercise on a warm day.

   _____

5. In some states, you _____ be 18 years old to drive.

   _____

 **TIMED WRITING: 45 minutes**

Write a process paragraph that explains the steps for choosing a special gift for someone you love. Before you begin to write, review the following time management strategy.

BRAINSTORMING: 5 minutes

Think about someone that you have bought a special gift for. Write down the gift that you chose and how you decided to buy it. Try to think of three or four steps that describe the process. Think of reason(s) that each step is important and write down the reasons.

OUTLINING: 5 minutes

Write an outline for your paragraph.

Topic Sentence

_____

_____

Supporting Sentences

Background information:

_____

_____

Step 1: _____

_____

_____

Step 2: _____

_____

_____

Step 3: _____

_____

_____

Step 4: _____

_____

_____

Concluding Sentence

_____

_____

WRITING: 25 minutes

Use your brainstorming notes and outline to write your first draft on a separate piece of paper.

When you have finished your first draft, check it for mistakes, using the checklist below.

Editor's Checklist

Put a check (✓) as appropriate.

☐ 1. Does the topic sentence tell what the task is?

☐ 2. Does the topic sentence contain a controlling idea?

☐ 3. Do the supporting sentences include a sequence of steps that give detailed information, background details, and the tools needed for the task?

☐ 4. Did you use time order words to separate the steps?

☐ 5. Did you use imperatives to give directions or instructions?

☐ 6. Did you use modals to express advice, necessity, and prohibitions?

☐ 7. Does the concluding sentence offer a suggestion or warning to help the reader do the task more easily?

☐ 8. Did you capitalize the first letter of each sentence and put end punctuation at the end?

Topics for Future Writing

1. Write a process paragraph on one of the following topics.

- How to obtain a driver's license
- How to find a house or apartment for rent
- How to throw a surprise birthday party for a friend
- How to play a video game

2. Interview a friend, classmate, or relative to learn how to do something. Take notes during the interview to use for your paragraph. Then write a process paragraph, explaining the steps to your reader.

Opinion Paragraphs

Unit Goals

Rhetorical Focus
- opinion organization
- using reasons to support an opinion

Language Focus:
- using *there is/there are* to introduce facts
- using *because of* and *because* to give reasons

In an opinion paragraph, the writer expresses and supports an opinion on a particular topic or issue. The writer must give reasons that help persuade the reader to agree with him or her.

Exercise 1   Thinking about the topic

Discuss the picture with a partner.

- Describe the picture. What kinds of natural beauty do you see?
- How might the natural landscape affect the people who live here?
- Would you like to live in a place like this? Why or why not?

Exercise 2   Reading about the topic

The author of this essay explains what he thinks makes Seattle a special place. Why does the author like Seattle so much?

City with a Gray-Green Heart

I think of Seattle as having a gray-green heart. It is a city shaped by nature, a city of snow-covered mountains, sparkling **glaciers**, and blue lakes. It has been called "America's Most Dynamic City," the "No. 1 City of the Future," and "America's Athens" by three major U.S. publications. But why has a town that is so far away from the nation's major power centers attracted so much attention? The answers may lie in Seattle's youthful energy and its scenery.

Seattle began as a wild **pioneer** town, and its energy continues in vigorous political activity and in the quiet creation of more millionaires **per capita** than any other urban area in the United States. Through six generations of gold seekers, **lumberjacks**, teachers, fishermen, airplane builders, and software inventors, we all share the feeling that living here is an adventure.

You would be **hard-pressed** to find a city as beautiful as Seattle. The Olympics and Cascade Mountains, Mount Baker and Mount Rainier, along with Lake Washington and Puget Sound, all offer spectacular views. The Space Needle **pokes up** over Queen Anne Hill, and the Lake Washington Ship Canal **shimmers** across the narrow waist of the city. Because of this magnificent natural landscape, people are both calm and yet energized as if they shared a feeling that Seattle is a place of unlimited possibility.

Rogers, J. W. *Seattle* (Adapted). Portland: Graphic Arts Center Publishing Company, 2006.

glaciers: rivers of ice
pioneer: early settler in a natural area
per capita: compared to the rest of the population

lumberjacks: workers who cut down trees for wood
hard-pressed: challenged
poke up: to stand
shimmer: to shine with a soft light

Exercise 3   **Understanding the text**

Write *T* for true or *F* for false for each statement.

_____ 1. The author lives in Seattle.

_____ 2. Seattle is a major power center in the world.

_____ 3. Seattle is a good place for people who have a sense of adventure.

_____ 4. Many Seattle residents are involved in politics.

_____ 5. There are beautiful views of mountains and water in Seattle.

Responding to the text

Write your answers to the questions in full sentences. Then discuss your answers with a partner.

1. What are some of the characteristics of the people of Seattle? _____

_____

_____

2. What did you learn about the history of Seattle from this text? _____

_____

_____

3. What are some of the natural features of the Seattle area? _____

_____

_____

4. Would you like to visit this city? Why or why not? _____

_____

_____

Freewriting

Write for ten minutes on the topic below. Express yourself as well as you can. Don't worry about making mistakes.

In "City with a Grey-Green Heart," the author writes about a city with natural beauty and youthful energy. What do you look for in a city? Describe the features of a city that would be perfect for you.

- What practical conveniences does the city have? (e.g., housing, jobs, transportation?)
- How does it look or feel?
- What entertainment, sports, or opportunities for fun are there?

> **In Part 2 you will ...**
> - learn about opinion organization.
> - brainstorm ideas and specific vocabulary to use in your writing.
> - create an outline for your opinion paragraph.

PART 2

Brainstorming and Outlining

WRITING TASK

In this unit, you will write an opinion paragraph about a city or town that you think provides a good quality of life.

Exercise 1 **Brainstorming ideas**

A. Review your freewriting exercise. Then brainstorm a list of three places where you would like to live. Give two or three reasons for each one.

Ideal places to live	Reasons
1.	
2.	
3.	

B. Choose the place that you would like to write about. Add one or two more reasons for why you would like to live there.

Brainstorming vocabulary

A. With a partner, discuss the meaning of the phrases in each category below. If you do not know a word, use your dictionary for help. Then brainstorm additional words for each category.

Attractions	Opportunities	Cost of living	People

temperate climate
beautiful scenery
interesting
   architecture
	low unemployment
	excellent colleges
	world-class
	   museums
		inexpensive
		   restaurants
		convenient public
		   transportation
		affordable housing
			talented cooks
			diverse
			   communities
			colorful
			   personalities

B. Select words from the chart above, including the words you added, and use them to write five sentences about the place you would like to live.

San Francisco has convenient public transportation.

_____

_____

_____

_____

_____

Rhetorical Focus

Opinion Organization

In an opinion paragraph, the writer presents an opinion and tries to persuade readers that the opinion is a good one. The writer tries to make readers agree with him or her.

Topic Sentence
- The topic sentence introduces the topic and states the writer's opinion about the topic.

Supporting Sentences
- The middle sentences give reasons that support the writer's opinion.
- Writers often use facts, explanations, and personal experiences to support their opinion.

Concluding Sentence
- The last sentence restates the writer's opinion in different words.
- It also comments on the opinion in some way.
- The concluding sentence sometimes summarizes the main reasons for the writer's opinion.

Exercise 3   **Reading a student paragraph**

Read the student paragraph. Why is Da Lat a paradise?

A Vietnamese Paradise

In Vietnam, the best place to spend a honeymoon is the beautiful mountain city called Da Lat. For many reasons, this romantic city has the perfect atmosphere for a new husband and wife to celebrate their marriage and plan their future. First of all, the scenery provides a beautiful setting for walking and talking. The climate is pleasant all year round because it is high above the ocean. Sometimes fog comes in and the city becomes mysterious and private. At other times, the sun shines, and Da Lat is cheerful and lively. There are beautiful gardens and lovely French colonial architecture. Young couples can walk along the boulevards in the shade of tall pine trees. They can sit on benches in the flower parks and hold hands. In addition, Dal Lat is fashionable. There are excellent hotels that have special rooms for honeymooners with candles and beautiful decorations. Also, the streets are full of activity, so the newlyweds can go out to one of the stylish restaurants that are open until late at night. The lights are soft, and the music is romantic. The newlyweds can eat delicious food, listen to music, and meet other young couples in love. Da Lat is the Vietnamese people's first choice for a honeymoon because it has lovely natural scenery, many romantic places to stay, and exciting things to do.

Examining the student paragraph

A. Respond to the paragraph by answering the questions below in full sentences.

1. How is the climate in Da Lat? _____

_____

_____

2. What activities can honeymooners enjoy in Da Lat? _____

_____

_____

3. What does the city look like? _____

_____

_____

4. What can people do at night in Da Lat? _____

_____

_____

5. Would you like to have a honeymoon in Da Lat? Explain. _____

_____

_____

B. Examine the organization of the essay by answering the questions below. Then compare your answers with a partner.

1. Underline the topic sentence. Which of the following statements best describes the main idea of the paragraph? (Choose one.)

_____ a. Da Lat is the perfect place to have a honeymoon.

_____ b. Da Lat is a popular place to have a honeymoon.

_____ c. Vietnam is a great place to live.

2. Which of the following reasons does the author use to support her opinion? (Choose all that apply.)

_____ a. the climate

_____ b. the reasonable cost of food and hotels

_____ c. the scenery and architecture

_____ d. the nightlife

_____ e. the transportation

3. Underline the concluding sentence twice. Which statement best describes the concluding sentence? (Choose one.)

_____ a. a description of how the climate of Da Lat is romantic

_____ b. a suggestion that the reader have a honeymoon in Da Lat

_____ c. a promise that Da Lat will not disappoint the reader

_____ d. a summary of the main reasons why Da Lat is a great place to have a honeymoon

Exercise 5   Writing an outline

Review your brainstorming ideas and your freewriting exercise. Then use the form below to write an outline for your paragraph. Remember to write your outline in note form.

Topic Sentence

State the topic and your opinion about the topic.

_____

_____

Supporting Sentences

What are some reasons for your opinion? Include notes about some of the following: attractions, opportunities, cost of living, and people.

_____

_____

_____

_____

Concluding Sentence

Restate your opinion and comment on it, or summarize the main reasons.

_____

_____

> **In Part 3 you will …**
> - learn to use facts, explanations, and experiences to support opinions.
> - write a first draft of your opinion paragraph.

PART 3

Developing Your Ideas

Exercise 1 **Reading a student paragraph**

Read the paragraph. Why does the author want to move?

Get Me Out of Here

Although many people say there are great opportunities in a big city, the life here is not good for me. First, people do not have enough free time because they are too busy with work and appointments. Parents and their children do not come home to eat lunch together. Some employees go to work before the sun comes up and return home after dark. Because of their schedules, families only spend time together on the weekend. Second, driving is necessary. Everyone must use a car to go to school or work or the store. I have to drive my children to school, and after school we go to soccer practice or to other activities. Because there is usually a lot of traffic, I have a lot of anxiety. Third, the cost of living is very expensive. Like many families, my family lives in an apartment because we cannot buy a house here. Also, people must spend a lot of money for entertainment. A visit to the aquarium costs twenty dollars for each ticket. In the future, I hope that I can live in a small town with friendly people. I want a house, a garden and a peaceful life. Maybe if I am lucky, my dream will come true, and I will move to a small town.

Exercise 2 **Examining the paragraph**

A. Respond to the paragraph by answering the questions in full sentences.

1. What is the author's opinion of city life? _____

_____

_____

2. What three main reasons does the author give to support her opinion?

_____

_____

3. What are some things that the author must do that she does not like to do?

_____

_____

4. Where does the author want to live? _____

_____

_____

5. Would you prefer to live in the city or the country? Why?

_____

_____

B. Examine the organization of the paragraph by answering the questions below. Then compare your answers with a partner.

1. Underline the topic sentence.

2. How many main reasons does the writer give? _____

3. Underline the concluding sentence twice. Does it restate the idea in the topic sentence? _____

4. Do you agree with any of the points the writer makes? Explain.

_____

_____

Rhetorical Focus

Using Reasons to Support an Opinion

There are often many different opinions about a certain topic. Therefore, writers must give reasons for their opinions in order to convince their readers. These supporting reasons are often in the form of facts, explanations, or experiences.

- A **fact** is a piece of information that people generally agree is true. In an opinion paragraph, a writer might use scientific, historical, or other types of facts.

- An **explanation** cannot be proven (like a fact can) but it still helps the reader understand why the writer holds a certain opinion.

> • An **experience** is something that happened to you or someone else. Writers often use experiences to show how they were influenced to think a certain way.
>
> Opinion: You have to be tough to live in Chicago.
> Fact: Winters in Chicago are very cold.
> Explanation: It is not easy to deal with those cold, windy days.
> Experience: My cousin once got frostbite while waiting at a bus stop.

Exercise 3   Identifying facts, explanations, and experiences

Read each opinion and the reasons that support it. Write *Fact*, *Explanation*, or *Experience* next to each reason.

1. Tokyo is the most technologically advanced city in Asia.

    _Fact_____ a. In Tokyo, most people have cell phones and many buildings are equipped with wireless technology.

    _____ b. Peoples' daily lives come to a halt if there is a blackout in Tokyo.

    _____ c. I rode the subway in Tokyo for many years, and it never broke down.

    _____ d. Some subway stations in Tokyo can handle more than a million passengers a day because of the use of computers.

2. Hawaii has the best surfing beaches in North America.

    _____ a. If you have never surfed in the Hawaiian Islands, you cannot be a world-class surfer because Hawaii is the benchmark by which other beaches are evaluated.

    _____ b. The winter waves in Oahu are higher than the summer waves, so serious surfers tend to spend time there during the winter months.

    _____ c. I got hooked on surfing after just one afternoon of surfing there.

    _____ d. Storm waves can rise as high as 20 feet with a face of up to 50 feet.

3. There is no better city to visit than Istanbul.

_____ a. People in Istanbul are friendly and always willing to help their neighbors.

_____ b. Bridges connect the neighborhoods of Istanbul so that it can exist in both Europe and Asia at the same time.

_____ c. I had the best meal of my life in a small café in Istanbul.

_____ d. Istanbul has a historically important location as a port city on the only route between the Mediterranean and the Black Sea.

Exercise 4   Using reasons to support an opinion

In each item, finish the first sentence by writing the name of a city or place that you know. Then add one reason (a fact, explanation, or experience) to support the opinion given.

1. I do not want to live in _____Chicago_____ because of the high cost of living. Housing in Chicago is very expensive. People sometimes work more than one job just to pay rent for a small apartment.

2. In my opinion, _____ has some of the friendliest people.

    _____

    _____

3. I believe that _____ is a very beautiful place to live.

    _____

    _____

4. _____ is a good place to raise a family for several reasons.

    _____

    _____

Exercise 5   Writing a first draft

Review your outline. Then write your first draft of an opinion paragraph about the best city to live in.

After you write your first draft, exchange it with a partner. Answer the questions on the checklist. You may also write comments or questions on your partner's draft. Then read your partner's comments on your first draft, and revise it as necessary.

Editor's Checklist

Put a check (✓) as appropriate. Write answers in complete sentences in the lines provided.

☐ 1. Does the paragraph have a topic sentence that expresses an opinion about the topic?

☐ 2. Does the paragraph include any facts to support the writer's opinion? What facts does it include? _____

_____

_____

☐ 3. Does the writer provide explanations that support the opinion?

☐ 4. Does the writer tell any experiences that support the opinion?

☐ 5. Does the writer need to provide more reasons to support the opinion? What kinds of reasons? _____

_____

_____

☐ 6. Does the paragraph have a concluding sentence that restates the writer's opinion and comments on it in some way?

In Part 4 you will …

- learn how to use *there is/there are* in statements.
- learn how to use *because of* or *because* to give reasons.
- edit your first draft for mistakes.

Editing Your Writing

Now that you have written a first draft, it is time to edit. Editing involves
making changes to your writing to improve it and correct mistakes.

Language Focus

Using *There Is/There Are*

Writers often use *there is/there are* to introduce facts.

There are harvest festivals every autumn.

There is a picturesque village in the mountains near Mexico City.

There are no mosquitoes at this altitude.

In a statement, a noun or a noun phrase follows *there is/there are*.
Use *there are* with plural nouns. Use *there is* with all other nouns.

There are tall <u>pine trees</u> lining the streets of Da Lat.(plural noun)

There is a large <u>lake</u> near Maracaibo. (singular noun)

There is <u>water</u> beyond the mountains. (noncount noun)

Use *no* after *there is/there are* to express a negative fact.

There is **no** snow.

There are **no** theaters in my hometown.

Exercise 1 **Practicing with *there is/there are***

Write *is* or *are* in the blanks to complete the sentences below.

1. There ____is____ a parade of children holding flowers.

2. There _____ a lot of music in the streets.

3. There _____ many nightclubs.

4. There _____ not many cars on the road, but you might see bicycles.

5. There _____ no airport in my city.

6. There _____ not much wind, so people prefer this beach.

Exercise 2 **Writing sentences with *there is/there are***

Rewrite the following sentences using *there is* or *there are*.

1. Bad weather is not in the South.

   <u>There is no bad weather in the South.</u>

2. Houses are not on the island.

_____

3. Colorful birds are in the jungle.

_____

4. Many international restaurants are downtown.

_____

5. Many vendors are on the beach.

_____

6. A lot of good seafood is along the coast.

_____

Language Focus

Using *Because Of* and *Because*

Use *because* or *because of* to give a reason. *Because of* is followed by a noun phrase.

People spend a lot of time outdoors **because of** <u>the mild climate</u>.

Because is followed by a complete sentence with its own subject and verb.

Tourists are attracted to the coast **because** <u>the fishing is fantastic</u>.

Note that in each example, *because of* and *because* give a reason after a statement.

Because of and *because* can also appear before the statement. When they come before, use a comma.

Because of the mild climate, people spend a lot of time outdoors.

Because the fishing is fantastic, tourists are attracted to the coast.

| Exercise 3 | **Practicing with *because of* and *because*** |

Use *because of* or *because* to complete each sentence below.

1. This city is a good place for young people _____<u>because of</u>_____ the world-class nightclubs.

2. There is a lot of diversity _____ many people from Europe and Asia moved to Brazil during the past two centuries.

3. Many people retire to warmer climates _____ the weather.

4. Gardening is popular there _____ the valley has ideal conditions for roses.

5. It is easy to get around the city _____ the government has improved the public transportation system.

6. A lot of people go there _____ the gourmet food.

Exercise 4 **Using *because of* and *because***

Finish each sentence with a phrase or a statement of your own.

1. I want to live in a big city because of _the cultural life._____

2. My city is beautiful because of _____

_____

3. My city is interesting because _____

_____

4. I would like to live in a small town because _____

_____

5. I do not want to live in a big city because of _____

_____

6. The best city to live in is _____ because of _____

_____

Exercise 5 **Editing a paragraph**

Read the following paragraph and correct mistakes with *there is/there are* and *because of* or *because*. There are seven mistakes.

The Beautiful Faces of Rio de Janeiro

I was very sad when I had to leave Rio de Janeiro because it is the best place on earth. Rio is important to me because of my family still lives there. However, I think anyone who moves there will agree it is a wonderful place. That is because Rio has something for every personality. First there is the people. Rio is famous because of many beautiful people live there, especially in the beach neighborhoods, such as Ipanema. The city is very fun during the Carnaval when Brazilians dress up in costumes and dance in the streets and nightclubs. Rio is also beautiful because its location. The city is on the Atlantic Ocean. There is a lot of beaches, and they are full of activity every day. The scenery is spectacular as well. You can see great geological formations, such as the granite mountain called Sugar Loaf, and on another peak named Corcovado, you can see an enormous statue that looks over the city. Brazil also has many varieties of music because the many cultures and traditions. Finally, there are also a place for people who enjoy tranquility. The botanical gardens are filled with exotic varieties of plants and animals. So Rio de Janeiro is a place with many different faces. It can be beautiful, crazy, and peaceful depending on your mood.

Exercise 6   **Editing your first draft and rewriting**

Review your paragraph for mistakes. Use the checklist below. Then write a final draft.

Editor's Checklist

Put a check (✓) as appropriate.

☐ 1. Did you use *there is/there are* to introduce the existence or location of something or someplace?

☐ 2. Did you use *because* to give reasons with statements?

☐ 3. Did you use *because of* to give reasons with noun phrases?

☐ 4. Did you capitalize the first letter of each sentence and put end punctuation at the end?

In Part 5 you will …

• review the elements of an opinion paragraph.
• practice writing with a time limit.

Putting It All Together

In this part of the unit, you will complete three exercises to improve your accuracy, write a timed paragraph to improve your fluency, and then explore topics for future writing.

Exercise 1   Identifying facts, explanations, and experiences

Read each opinion and the reasons that support it. Write *Fact*, *Explanation*, or *Experience* next to each reason.

1. The Guggenheim museum is the most interesting building in New York City.

    _____ a. The tilted corkscrew shape of the building is unlike anything else in the city.

    _____ b. It was designed by the architect, Frank Loyd Wright.

    _____ c. The first time I saw the Guggenheim, I was so amazed that I spent an hour just looking at the building from the outside.

    _____ d. Many visitors have trouble focusing on the artwork because they are distracted by the intensity of the architecture.

2. People spend too much money on personal appearance.

    _____ a. People spend billions annually on cosmetics.

    _____ b. People want to look good, but they are spending money that could be used for more important purposes such as education or a home.

    _____ c. Cosmetic surgery is becoming more and more costly as the variety of procedures increases.

    _____ d. My brother-in-law had to work overtime because his wife spent a lot of money on clothes, and jewelry, so he owed a lot of money on his credit cards.

3. Water is our most important natural resource.

    _____ a. What would happen in your house if you lost water for one day?

    _____ b. The human body is 98 percent water.

    _____ c. Lack of fresh drinking water causes major health crises in some countries every year.

    _____ d. Not only is water important for drinking, washing and bathing, it is also important for growing food.

Exercise 2 Writing sentences with *there is/there are*

Rewrite the following sentences using sentences with *there is/there are*.

1. Whales are in Puget Sound in the summer.

   _____

2. Gold exists in Siberia.

   _____

3. Penguins are not in Florida.

   _____

4. No cure exists for cancer.

   _____

5. Many stories exist about the first blue-eyed tribes that lived in Argentina.

   _____

6. Beautiful terraced hillsides are in China.

   _____

Exercise 3 Using *because of* and *because*

Complete each sentence with *because of* or *because*.

1. Many people learn English _____ their jobs.

2. Many young people go out in the evening _____ they like to listen to music.

3. Our food is hot _____ we use a lot of chilies.

4. Most people do not have private boats _____ they are very expensive.

5. We won the game _____ the other goalie's error.

6. A lot of people become English teachers _____ the opportunities to travel.

TIMED WRITING: 45 minutes

Write an opinion paragraph about what you think is the best age to get married. Before you begin to write, review the following time management strategy.

BRAINSTORMING: 5 minutes

Write down three or four ages that people get married. Then think of reasons why each might be good. Then choose the best age for your paragraph.

OUTLINING: 5 minutes

Write an outline for your paragraph.

Topic Sentence

State the topic and your opinion about the topic.

_____

_____

Supporting Sentences

Facts: _____

_____

_____

Explanations: _____

_____

_____

Experiences: _____

_____

_____

Concluding Sentence

Restate your opinion and comment on it, or summarize the main reasons.

_____

_____

WRITING: 25 minutes

Use your brainstorming notes and outline to write your first draft on a separate piece of paper.

When you have finished your first draft, check it for errors, using the checklist below.

Editor's Checklist

Put a check (✓) as appropriate.

☐ 1. Does the topic sentence state your opinion about the topic?

☐ 2. Did you include facts, explanations, and personal experiences to support your opinion?

☐ 3. Does the paragraph have a concluding sentence that restates your opinion?

☐ 4. Did you use *there is/there are* to introduce facts?

☐ 5. Did you use *because of* and *because* correctly when giving reasons?

☐ 6. Did you capitalize the first letter of each sentence and put end punctuation at the end?

Topics for Future Writing

1. **Write an opinion paragraph on one of the following topics.**

   - What is the best job for you? Why?
   - Is it a good idea to live with relatives?
   - Are pets good companions?
   - What changes would you like to see made to the educational system?

2. **Interview a friend, classmate, or relative about his or her views on one of the topics above. Take notes during the interview to use for your paragraph. Then write an opinion paragraph on one of the topics above, but from your friend's point of view.**

Narrative Paragraphs

Unit Goals

Rhetorical Focus
- narrative organization
- using sensory and emotional details

Language Focus:
- showing order of events in narrative paragraphs
- showing simultaneous events
- forming and using the simple past
- forming and using the past continuous

PART 1

Stimulating Ideas

In narrative writing, the writer tells a story that sets the background for an event, describes the event, and often comments on the event. In this chapter, you will write a narrative paragraph that tells the story of an event in your life.

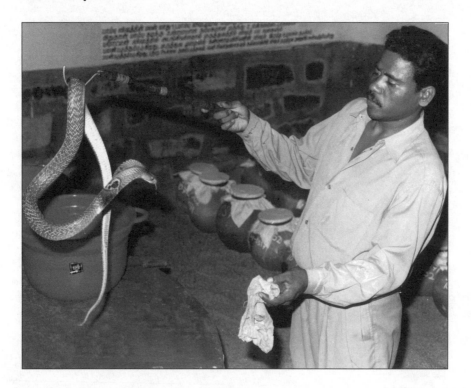

Exercise 1 | Thinking about the topic

Discuss the picture with a partner.

- Describe the man in the photograph.
- How does he feel?
- What do you think he is doing?
- What might happen to him?
- Do you think people are brave if they feel fear when they do something difficult or dangerous?

Exercise 2 | Reading about the topic

The author, who is working in West Africa, describes a frightening experience at a dinner party. A deadly poisonous snake called a Green Mamba has entered the house and chased the guests outside. The host has summoned "the snake-man" to come and take the unwelcome visitor away. What happens next?

The Snake-Man

"There's a good boy," the snake-man said softly. "There's a clever boy. There's a lovely fellow. You mustn't get excited. Keep calm and everything's going to be all right." As he was speaking, he was slowly lowering the end of the **pole** until the forked **prongs** were about twelve inches above the middle of the snake's body. "There's a lovely fellow," he whispered. "There's a good kind little chap. Keep still now, my beauty. Keep still, my pretty. Daddy's not going to hurt you."

Then wham, the rubber prongs came down right across the snake's body about midway along its length and pinned it to the floor. All I could see was a green blur as the snake **thrashed** around furiously in an effort to free itself. But the snake-man kept up the pressure on the prongs and the snake was trapped.

…

Then at last the prongs were right behind the head itself, **pinning** it down, and at that point the snake-man reached forward with one **gloved** hand and **grasped** the snake very firmly by the neck. He threw away the pole. He took the sack off his shoulder with his free hand. He lifted the great still twisting length of the deadly green snake and pushed the head into the sack. Then he let go the head and bundled the rest of the creature in the closed sack. The sack started jumping about as though there were fifty angry rats inside it, but the snake-man was now totally relaxed and he held the sack casually in one hand as if it contained no more than a few pounds of potatoes.

Dahl, R. *Going Solo*. New York: Farrar, Straus & Giroux, LLC, 1986.

pole: a long slender rod
prongs: pointed ends of a tool
thrash: move around wildly

pin: hold firmly against the ground
gloved: with a glove on
grasp: hold firmly

Exercise 3 **Understanding the text**

Write *T* for true or *F* for false for each statement.

_____ 1. The snake-man talked to the snake.

_____ 2. The snake-man pinned the snake to the floor with his bare hands.

_____ 3. The snake was moving around as the snake-man held it in his hand.

_____ 4. The snake jumped around after it was in the sack.

_____ 5. The snake-man seemed afraid as he held the sack with the snake in it.

Responding to the text

Write your answers to the questions in full sentences. Then discuss your answers with a partner.

1. What did the snake-man do to keep the snake calm while he was preparing to catch it? _____

    _____

    _____

2. What did the snake do after the snake-man caught it? _____

    _____

    _____

3. How do you think the snake-man felt while he was catching the snake? Explain. _____

    _____

    _____

4. Why didn't the snake-man just kill the snake? _____

    _____

    _____

Freewriting

Write for ten minutes on the topic below. Express yourself as well as you can. Don't worry about making mistakes.

In "The Snake-Man" the author describes an experience that required courage. Have you ever done something that challenged you? It does not have to be something dangerous; it can be something that simply made you nervous, such as speaking in front of an audience. Think about the following questions as you write:

- What did you do?
- Why did you do it?
- How did it make you feel?
- What did it teach you about yourself?

In Part 2 you will …

- learn about narrative organization.
- brainstorm ideas and specific vocabulary to use in your writing.
- create an outline for your narrative paragraph.

PART 2

Organizing Your Ideas

✍ WRITING TASK

In this unit, you will write a narrative paragraph about a challenge that you have faced.

Exercise 1 **Brainstorming ideas**

A. Review your freewriting exercise. Then choose two experiences you have had that challenged you or required courage. Write them in the chart below. Then answer the questions for each experience in note form.

	Experience 1	Experience 2
1. When did the experience take place? How long did the experience last?		
2. Where did the experience take place?		
3. What clear and specific memories do you have of the experience?		

B. Choose one experience from the chart that you would most like to write about. Often a single event in a single place is easier to describe than something that took place over a long period of time or at many places. Describe to your partner the event you chose.

Exercise 2 **Brainstorming vocabulary**

A. With a partner, brainstorm additional descriptive words to complete each sentence.

1. I was in a/an _____ place.
   (scary, elegant, enormous, _____strange_____, _____faraway_____)

2. I felt _____.
   (nervous, important, numb, _____, _____)

3. I _____.
   (ran, cried, fell, _____, _____)

4. The experience _____ me.
   (thrilled, matured, motivated, _____, _____)

5. I gained a lot of _____ from this experience.
   (confidence, knowledge, friends, _____, _____)

B. Choose five words you wrote in Part A and use them to write five additional sentences about your experience.

1. My body felt numb. _____

2. _____

3. _____

4. _____

5. _____

6. _____

Rhetorical Focus

Narrative Organization

A narrative paragraph tells a story. Like other kinds of paragraphs you have learned about in this book, it has a topic sentence, supporting sentences, and a concluding sentence.

Topic Sentence
- The topic sentence tells the reader what the story will be about.
- It may also tell when and where the story took place.
- The topic sentence should capture the reader's interest.

Supporting Sentences
- The supporting sentences tell the details of the story, including the sequence of events.
- They also include sensory details, such as what the author saw, heard, smelled, or tasted.
- Supporting sentences may also tell about the writer's feelings during the events.

Concluding Sentence
- The concluding sentence "wraps up" the story. It may include a comment about why the experience was important or how the writer felt after it.

| Exercise 3 | **Reading a student paragraph** |

Read the student paragraph. What made the hamburger memorable?

The Best Hamburger of My Life

When I was thirteen years old, I had a great surprise at the Grand Hotel in Toronto. My favorite soccer team was visiting from Mexico, so I went to the hotel to get autographs from some of the players. When I got there, I waited outside for a long time because I was very nervous. Finally, I told my legs to start moving, and I went up to my favorite striker, Sergio Verdirame, and asked for his autograph. My voice was trembling, but I controlled it. He stopped to listen to me, and then an amazing thing happened. He invited me to his table for dinner. I could not believe it! Suddenly I was sitting across the table from Sergio Verdirame! I ordered a big hamburger with everything on it except onions. When the food came, my hands were shaking, and I could not eat or talk. After a while, I took a deep breath and said to myself, "Hey, this happens just once in your life." I got rid of my nerves and started talking with the team and enjoying my hamburger. They were really great guys, and we had a good time laughing and joking together. That was the most delicious hamburger I ever ate in my life because I was eating it with my idol.

A. Respond to the paragraph by answering the questions below in full sentences.

1. Why did the writer go to the hotel? _____

    _____

2. What did he do after he got there? Why? _____

    _____

    _____

3. What kind of challenge did the writer face? Was it physical or emotional?

    Explain. _____

    _____

4. How did the writer deal with the challenge? _____

    _____

    _____

5. Have you ever had a similar challenge? Explain. _____

    _____

    _____

B. Examine the organization of the paragraph by answering the questions below. Then compare your answers with a partner.

1. Underline the topic sentence. What information appears in the topic

    sentence? _____

    _____

2. Read the following events from the story. Number them in the order in which they occurred.

    _____ a. The writer ordered a hamburger.

    _____ b. The writer was very nervous and his hands were shaking.

    _____ c. The writer asked the soccer player for his autograph.

    _____ d. Sergio Verdirame invited the writer to have dinner.

    _____ e. The writer overcame his fear and enjoyed his dinner.

3. In the concluding sentence, the writer explains what made him happiest. Which sentence best describes his final comment?

    a. He was able to eat a very good hamburger.

    b. He was able to spend time with his favorite soccer player.

    c. He was able to overcome his fear of speaking to his heroes.

    d. He finally got an autograph from his favorite player.

Writing an outline

Review your brainstorming ideas and your freewriting exercise. Then use the form below to write an outline for your narrative paragraph. Remember to write your outline in note form.

Topic Sentence

What is the story about? Where and when did it take place? _____

_____

_____

Supporting Sentences

What happened first? _____

_____

_____

What happened next? _____

_____

_____

What else happened? _____

_____

_____

_____

_____

How did the experience end? _____

_____

_____

Concluding Sentence

What was important about the experience? How did it affect you? _____

_____

_____

In Part 3 you will ...

- learn to use sensory and emotional details in a narrative paragraph.
- learn to show the order of events in a narrative paragraph.
- write a first draft of your narrative paragraph.

Exercise 1   **Reading a student paragraph**

Read the student paragraph. How did the author feel just before his wild experience?

Something Wild

For my 25th birthday, my favorite uncle gave me a gift certificate to go skydiving at a special place near Miami. I was happy because I wanted to do something wild. On the day of my jump, I woke up with a crazy feeling in my stomach. I could not eat breakfast because of the nerves. After we arrived at the place, I had to sign a lot of papers because of the risk involved. I signed them quickly because I did not want to think about the danger. Before I knew it, I was on the plane with my parachute on my back. The only thing I could think was, "What am I doing?" One of the staff opened the door of the plane and told me to get ready. I put my right foot over the edge and waited for the signal … "three, two, one …" and then I was free falling, going down at almost two hundred kilometers per hour. I was shouting, and I could feel adrenaline running through me. Nearby, there was another guy taking photos. I like to take photos too. Then the parachute opened, and the next five minutes were the most incredible moments of my life. I was floating completely free, like a bird. All my problems were gone, and I could see the curve of the earth, the ocean, and faraway clouds off the shore. It was awesome. Those wonderful moments helped me to realize that I am the kind of person who likes to take risks, and I hope I always will be.

Analyzing the student paragraph

A. Respond to the paragraph by answering the questions below in full sentences.

1. Where was the author when he had the experience? _____
   _____

2. Why did the author jump out of an airplane? _____
   _____
   _____

3. How did the author feel while in the air? _____
   _____
   _____

4. Would you like to do the same thing? Why or why not? _____
   _____
   _____

B. Examine the organization of the essay by answering the questions below. Then compare your answers with a partner.

1. Underline the topic sentence. What background details does it include?
   _____
   _____

2. How does the author feel about jumping out of an airplane? Why do you
   think he feels this way? _____
   _____

3. Does the event take place in one location? _____

4. Cross out one sentence that is not directly related to the topic sentence of
   the paragraph.

5. Underline the concluding sentence twice. What did the author learn from his
   experience? _____
   _____
   _____

Rhetorical Focus

Using Sensory and Emotional Details

In order to make a narrative paragraph interesting, writers include sensory details and emotional details that help the reader share the experience of the story.

- Sensory details give information about how something looks, smells, tastes, feels or what it sounds like.

  My teeth were chattering, and my legs felt like jelly.
  The morning sun warmed my back.

- Emotional details help the reader understand the writer's feelings.

  Suddenly, my fear vanished, and I felt confident as I looked out at the crowd.
  The sight filled me with excitement.

Exercise 3 Identifying sensory and emotional details

Read the sentences below. Write an *S* next to sentences that have sensory details. Write an *E* next to the sentences that have emotional details.

__S__ 1. The morning mist brought in the smell of the ocean.

____ 2. We were very nervous, so we called the police.

____ 3. I had never felt such happiness.

____ 4. The dates were sticky and sweet, and they were a delicious compliment to the hot, bitter tea.

____ 5. I felt a sharp pain in my ankle, and I recognized the sting of a jellyfish.

____ 6. We could hear the roar of the waterfall for a long time before we actually saw it.

Exercise 4 Practicing with sensory details

Use sensory details to support the following sentences.

1. Our guide had an interesting fashion sense.
   He wore the same khaki pants every day, but his shirts always had
   colorful patterns of flowers, dancers, or other tropical scenes.

2. We ate a wonderful meal.

   _____

   _____

3. The flower garden was delightful.

_____

_____

4. The alley had not been taken care of for many years and it was in bad shape.

_____

_____

5. My father taught me to swim in a river behind our house.

_____

_____

6. My mother's kitchen was everyone's favorite room.

_____

_____

Exercise 5 **Practicing with emotional details**

Use emotional details to support the following sentences.

1. I would like to forget my first job interview.
   I was so nervous my hands were wet, and so was my shirt.

2. I met my girlfriend on the Internet.

   _____

   _____

3. At first, I did not like the new puppy, but after awhile I changed my mind.

   _____

   _____

4. I began to walk down the aisle towards my future husband.

   _____

   _____

5. I walked into the cold dark cave.

   _____

   _____

6. The test was over, and I had earned the highest score.

   _____

   _____

Showing Order of Events in Narrative Paragraphs

Writers of narrative essays use sequence words and expressions to clarify the order of events in a story.

The following sequence words are used when events happen in chronological (time) order. They often begin sentences.

next	after that	afterwards	then	later
finally	eventually	a little while later	soon	

We unpacked the car and set up our tent. **After that**, we built a fire and cooked our food.

Our entire family squeezed into the car, and **soon** we were on our way.

Showing Simultaneous Events

Writers use the following words and expressions to show that two events occurred at the same time.

meanwhile	while	at the same time that

I made coffee. **Meanwhile**, my brother tried to distract our mother.

I was planning a surprise party **at the same time that** I was getting ready to move.

<u>Exercise 6</u>   **Identifying order of events**

Read the following sentences. Then number them in the order you think they occurred. Use the sequence words and phrases as clues.

<u>1</u>   a. A few years ago, my two older brothers and I went trekking in the mountains.

_____ b. Finally, I found the muddy trail, and we made it back to our base camp.

_____ c. Soon we were hiking through thick pine forests.

_____ d. We set out from our base camp on a bright winter morning.

_____ e. After that experience, I realized it is very important to be careful when hiking in the mountains.

_____ f. A little while later, we stopped to eat, and my oldest brother said we should turn around because we were losing the trail in the snow.

_____ g. Eventually, it began to snow, and visibility became poor.

_____ h. Going back down the mountain was harder because it was icy and slippery, and we could not find the way. We became tired, cold and thirsty.

Exercise 7   Writing a first draft

Review your outline. Then write the first draft of a narrative essay about a challenge you faced.

Exercise 8   Peer editing a first draft

After you write your first draft, exchange it with a partner. Answer the questions on the checklist. You may also write comments or questions on your partner's draft. Then read your partner's comments on your first draft, and revise it as necessary.

Editor's Checklist

Put a check (✓) as appropriate. Write answers in complete sentences in the lines provided.

☐ 1. Does the paragraph have a topic sentence that tells what the story will be about?

☐ 2. Do the supporting sentences tell the details of the story?

☐ 3. Does the writer use sensory and emotional details? If so, what sensory and emotional details are included? _____

_____

_____

☐ 4. Does the writer use sequence words and transition words to explain the order of the events in the story? If so, which ones? _____

_____

_____

☐ 5. Does the paragraph have a concluding sentence that "wraps up" the story? Does it include a comment about the experience? If so, what is the comment? _____

_____

_____

In Part 4 you will ...

- learn about simple past tense verbs.
- learn about past continuous verbs.
- edit your first draft for mistakes.

Editing Your Writing

Now that you have written a first draft, it is time to edit. Editing involves making changes to your writing to improve it and correct mistakes.

Language Focus

Using the Simple Past

- Use the simple past to tell about actions and events that started and finished in the past.

  Dalia **walked** home quickly that night.
  Ronald **studied** all night for that exam.

Forming the Simple Past

- Add *-d* or *-ed* to the base form of most regular verbs to form the simple past.

  In 2003, I **celebrated** Christmas with my family in Baranquilla.
  I **graduated** from high school in 2001.

- Some verbs are irregular in the simple past.

  Eliza and her sister **spent** all their money.
  I **met** my husband at the airport on New Year's Day.

- To form a negative statement in the simple past with a regular or irregular verb, use *did not* followed by the base form of the verb.

  I **did not fall** off the cliff.
  I **did not waste** any money.

- The verb *be* has two past forms. *Was* and *were*.

  Doug **was** a good father.
  Scott and Eric **were** anxious.

- To form negative statements with *be* in the simple past, use *not* after *was* or *were*.

  Eliza **was not** nervous.
  They **were not** generous people.

Affirmative Statements		
SUBJECT	BASE FORM OF VERB + -D/-ED	
I You He She It We You They	waited	patiently.

Negative Statements			
SUBJECT	DID + NOT	BASE FORM OF VERB	
I You He She It We You They	did not	wait	patiently.

Affirmative Statements		
SUBJECT	WAS/WERE	
I	was	
You	were	
He She It	was	beautiful.
We You They	were	

Negative Statements		
SUBJECT	WAS/WERE + NOT	
I	was not	
You	were not	
He She It	was not	beautiful.
We You They	were not	

Exercise 1 Using simple past tense verbs

Complete the following sentences with past tense verbs.

1. I _____was_____ interested in Astronomy.

2. We _____ about our plans.

3. She _____ an umbrella, some sandwiches, and a thermos of hot, sweet tea.

4. We _____ for help, and a helicopter _____ to rescue us.

5. We _____ the roasted pig with fried plantains and Arepas.

6. There _____ 122 people at the wedding.

7. After I _____ my host family, I _____ less worried.

8. We _____ to the top of a mountain where we _____ an ancient temple.

Read the following paragraph and correct mistakes with the simple past tense. There are ten mistakes.

> Two years ago, my friends and I decide to go to a special temple in my country. We wake up very early in the morning that day. We brought some fruit and drinks for breakfast. After we ate our fruits, we want to climb the mountain. We got to the temple about 10 a.m. It was very beautiful. We stay there and talked, but after a while, we wanted to hike some more. We did not brought food, but we had some water, and we started climbing. We become tired, but we did not wanted to stop. We was thirsty too, but we did not had enough water. Finally we met some people and they gave us drinks and helped us. That day, I learn to be very careful when I go hiking in the mountains.

Language Focus

Using the Past Continuous

- Use the past continuous to describe an event that was already in progress when another event occurred or interrupted the first event.

  My brother and I **were watching** TV when we heard a crash.
  The car **was moving** slowly, so I had plenty of time to cross the street.

- Use the past continuous to tell about two or more activities that were in progress at the same time.

  She **was running** while **talking** on the cell phone.
  Some teenagers **were splashing** and **shouting** at each other.

Forming the Past Continuous

- To form the past continuous, use *was/were* and the base form of the verb + *ing*

  I **was living** in Washington at the time.

- To form negative statements in the past continuous, use *not* between *was/were* and the verb + *ing*.

  We **were not laughing** at the comedian's jokes**.**

- ⚠ We do not usually use stative verbs (*be, know, understand, see, believe*) in the past continuous. Use the simple past instead.

Affirmative Statements				Negative Statements		
SUBJECT	WAS/WERE	BASE FORM OF VERB + ING		SUBJECT	WAS/WERE + NOT	BASE FORM OF VERB + ING
I	was			I	was not	
You	were			You	were not	
He She It	was	watching.		He She It	was not	watching.
We You They	were			We You They	were not	

Exercise 3 **Using the past continuous**

Answer the following questions with sentences that use the past continuous.

1. What were you doing yesterday at this time?

   I was shopping for a gift for my sister.

2. What were you doing last night at 6 p.m.?

   _____

3. What were you doing this morning at 10 a.m.?

   _____

4. What were you doing last year at this time?

   _____

5. What were you thinking about while you were coming to school today?

   _____

Exercise 4 **Identifying when to use the past continuous**

Underline the verbs in each sentence. Then rewrite the sentences replacing the simple past with the past continuous where it is more appropriate.

1. I talked to my friend while the teacher explained the grammar, so I did not understand it.

   I was talking to my friend when the teacher was explaining the grammar,

   so I did not understand it.

2. I lived in Paris when I had a terrible car accident.

   _____

3. I worked on my paper and watched the game when he called.

_____

4. A stranger stood in the doorway when we arrived home.

_____

5. We drove to the hospital when my wife told the taxi driver to stop the car.

_____

6. In those days I worked and went to school, so I didn't have much free time.

_____

Exercise 5 **Editing a paragraph**

Read the following paragraph and correct mistakes with the simple past and the past continuous. There are nine mistakes.

When I was a university student about two years ago, I enrolled in a scuba diving course. My scuba diving teacher was having a big surprise: I wasn't knowing how to swim. In fact, I had a big fear of water. When I was a child, my parents tried to help me, so they make me take many swimming courses. Although I try hard, I did not learning to swim. When I enrolled in the scuba diving course, I was still afraid of water. Every day when I entered the swimming pool, I battle with my fear. Fortunately, my courage won every time. Finally, one day while I practicing my dive, I realized that I was do very well. So, finally, after six months of hard work, I completed the course. It is true that I was always the worst of the group, but in my own evaluation, I was a champion because I conquer my fear of water. For me, this experience was very important. It was a test of courage, and I passed it.

Editing your first draft and rewriting

Review your paragraph for mistakes. Use the checklist below. Then write a final draft.

Grammar Checklist

Put a check (✓) as appropriate.

☐ 1. Did you use the simple past to express events that started and finished in the past?

☐ 2. Did you check for correct irregular verb forms?

☐ 3. Did you use the past continuous to show simultaneous or interrupted actions?

☐ 4. Did you capitalize the first letter of each sentence and put end punctuation at the end?

In Part 5 you will …

• review the elements of a narrative paragraph.
• write a timed narrative paragraph.

PART 5

Putting It All Together

In this part of the unit, you will complete three exercises to improve your accuracy, write a timed paragraph to improve your fluency, and explore topics for future writing.

Exercise 1 Identifying sensory and emotional details

Read the sentences below. Write an *S* next to sentences that include sensory details. Write an *E* next to sentences that include emotional details.

_____ 1. Olivia reached for the doorknob, and it was burning hot.

_____ 2. Ricky and I arrived around 8:00, and we were happy to be home.

_____ 3. We were greeted by a large man with long black hair.

_____ 4. I was shocked and disappointed by the results.

_____ 5. My mother always smelled like flowery perfume.

_____ 6. The news left us saddened and worried about the future.

Exercise 2 Identifying order of events

Read the following sentences. Then number them in the order you think they occurred. Use the sequence words and phrases as clues.

_____ a. For years, I did not know what to do with my life, but after I decided to become a helicopter pilot, I became very dedicated to my goal.

_____ b. At the beginning, I delivered groceries in my truck.

_____ c. After that, I had to get a visa and prepare to come to the U.S.

_____ d. Next, I made a plan to get the money for my training. I became a truck driver and drove all over Japan for five years.

_____ e. First, I did some research and found out that it would cost a lot of money.

_____ f. Finally, I was ready to take my training. Someone advised me to do a program in the U.S. because it was not as expensive, so I decided to come here even though I needed more English.

_____ g. Now, I am in the U.S. I go to school to study English. At the same time, I take flying lessons.

_____ h. Later, I got another job delivering fuel to gas stations. I lived in my truck to save money.

_____ i. Finally, I am learning to pilot a helicopter, and soon I will be ready to fly solo. I know that I will reach my goal in two years.

Read the following paragraph and correct mistakes with the simple past and the past continuous. There are ten mistakes.

Facing Danger in French Guiana

Three years ago, I was living in an exciting and adventurous place: French Guiana. My husband and I own a lovely house that was right next to the jungle. Many animals lived there, such as crocodiles, monkeys, poisonous spiders, jaguars, tigers, and snakes. People often warn us that our house was too close to the jungle, but we enjoying the house so much that we decided to stay. Then one morning I had a frightening adventure. I was plan to go for a swim in the pool. I put on my swimming suit, and went outside and start to cross the patio. I was take off my jacket to dive in the water when suddenly, I had a big surprise. A big snake was swim in my pool and move quickly towards me. I could not breathe. It seemed as though he staring at me for a long time. I ran into the house to call the police. When they arrive, the snake was gone. That day I learned to never jump in that pool before inspecting it for visitors.

TIMED WRITING: 45 minutes

Write a narrative paragraph about something that happened to you while you were on a trip. Before you begin to write, review the following time management strategy.

Step 1   **BRAINSTORMING: 5 minutes**

Make a list of recent trips you have taken. Write down some of the things that you did on those trips, people you met, and things that you saw. Keep adding to your list until you decide on a specific incident that you would like to write about.

OUTLINING: 5 minutes

Write an outline for your paragraph.

Topic Sentence

What is the story about? _____

_____

Where did it take place? _____

_____

Supporting Sentences

What happened first? _____

_____

_____

What happened next? _____

_____

_____

What else happened? _____

_____

_____

_____

_____

How did the experience end? _____

_____

_____

How did you feel during the experience? _____

_____

_____

Concluding Sentence

What was important about the experience? How did it affect you? _____

_____

_____

WRITING: 25 minutes

Use your brainstorming notes and outline to write your first draft on a separate piece of paper.

EDITING: 10 minutes

When you have finished your first draft, check it for mistakes, using the checklist below.

Editor's Checklist

Put a check (✓) as appropriate.

☐ 1. Does the paragraph have a title?

☐ 2. Does the paragraph have a topic sentence that tells what the story will be about?

☐ 3. Does the paragraph have background information?

☐ 4. Does the paragraph give the events of the story?

☐ 5. Are there sensory and/or emotional details?

☐ 6. Does the paragraph use sequence words and/or other transition words to show the order of events?

☐ 7. Did you use simple past and past continuous verbs in the correct form?

☐ 8. Did you include a concluding sentence that "wraps up" the story? Does it tell how the experience affected you?

Topics for Future Writing

1. **Write a narrative paragraph on one of the following topics.**

   • How you met someone who is important to you
   • The last time you celebrated a special holiday
   • A special memory from your childhood
   • A funny or embarrassing incident

2. **Interview a friend, classmate, or relative about something interesting that happened to him or her. Take notes during the interview. Then write a narrative paragraph about your friend's experience.**

Appendices

Appendix I: **The Writing Process**

1. Brainstorming

Before you begin to write, gather information about the topic. Then brainstorm ideas and vocabulary related to the topic. Read your assignment carefully so that your finished product will meet your instructor's expectations.

> ▶ **Strategies:** Read about the topic and discuss it with your classmates. Look at pictures or diagrams to help you come up with ideas.

2. Creating an Outline

Decide which ideas you will use in your essay. Cluster ideas into logical parts. This may be in the form of a chart, a web, or a list of main ideas. Write an outline or plan for your paper.

> ▶ **Strategies:** Look at models that are similar to the writing that you want to do. Learn ways to organize and sequence your ideas. Create a visual plan for your paper.

3. Writing a First Draft

Expand your outline into a draft by rewriting your notes into full sentences. At this stage, don't worry about mistakes. When you have finished, ask a classmate to read your work and give you feedback.

> ▶ **Strategies:** Evaluate your outline as you write. Take out ideas that do not support your main idea; add clarification or examples. Check your work to make sure your writing is clear and accomplishes the goals of the assignment.

4. Editing

Now apply your knowledge of grammar and mechanics, and correct any mistakes that you notice. Review the feedback you received from your classmates.

> ▶ **Strategies:** Separate yourself from the ideas so that you can focus on clarity at the sentence level. If possible, put your paper aside for a few hours before you edit. Read your essay sentence by sentence. (Some writers read a paper backwards so as not to be distracted by content.)

5. Writing a Final Draft and Submitting Your Work

Rewrite your draft so that it looks neat and has all the features of a finished college paper. Some writers type their papers; others write by hand.

> ▶ **Strategies:** Make sure your paper has the correct format. Make sure your name and the date are on the paper, and that there is a title.

Appendix II: **Elements of Punctuation**

Commas (,)

A comma is used to separate information from other parts of the sentence.

1. A comma is used to separate items in a series. Use *and* before the last item if listing three or more items.
   - We made rice, chicken, salad, and cake.

2. A comma is used to separate an introductory word or phrase.
   - At the end of the day, my husband and I sit on the sofa and talk about our day.

3. A comma is used to separate two sentences when there is a conjunction such as *and*, *but*, or *so* that shows a relationship between them.
   - The temperature was below freezing, but we were warm.

Periods (.)

Periods are used to mark the end of a sentence.

   - She speaks four languages.

Apostrophes (')

Apostrophes are used to show possession.

1. When a noun is singular, add an apostrophe and *s* to show possession. In the first example, the writer has one cousin.
   - We went to my cousin's house.

2. When a noun is plural, put the apostrophe after the plural *s*. In the next example, the writer has more than one cousin.
   - We went to my cousins' house.

3. When a noun ends in *s*. You may add the apostrophe + *s* after the final *s* or just the apostrophe.
   - My boss' car was ridiculously expensive.
   - My boss's car was ridiculously expensive.

4. Apostrophes are also used to show contractions. (Note, however, that contractions are not appropriate in academic writing.)
   - Scott doesn't have any hair.

Quotation Marks ("...")

Quotation marks are used to show that you are repeating or quoting someone else's words.

Put quotation marks around only the exact words you take from someone else's speech or writing. Use a comma to separate the quote from the rest of the sentence.

   - I heard him say, "Don't worry about the rebate, Mr. Noor. I will take care of it."

Appendix III: **Glossary**

Adapted from the **Grammar Sense** *Glossary of Grammar Terms*

action verb A verb that describes a thing that someone or something does. An action verb does not describe a state or condition.

> Sam **rang** the bell.
> It **rains** a lot here.

active sentence In active sentences, the agent (the noun that is performing the action) is in subject position and the receiver (the noun that receives or is a result of the action) is in object position. In the following sentence, the subject **Alex** performed the action, and the object **letter** received the action.

> Alex mailed the letter.

adjective A word that describes or modifies the meaning of a noun.

> the **orange** car   a **strange** noise

adverb A word that describes or modifies the meaning of a verb, another adverb, an adjective, or a sentence. Many adverbs answer such questions as *How? When? Where?* or *How often?* They often end in **-ly.**

> She ran **quickly**.   She ran **very** quickly.
> a **really** hot day   **Maybe** she'll leave.

adverbial phrase A phrase that functions as an adverb.

> Amy spoke **very softly**.

affirmative statement A sentence that does not have a negative verb.

> Linda went to the movies.

agreement The subject and verb of a clause must agree in number. If the subject is singular, the verb form is also singular. If the subject is plural, the verb form is also plural.

> **He comes** home early.   **They come** home early.

article The words **a, an,** and **the** in English. Articles are used to introduce and identify nouns.

> **a** potato   **an** onion   **the** supermarket

auxiliary verb A verb that is used before main verbs (or other auxiliary verbs) in a sentence. Auxiliary verbs are usually used in questions and negative sentences. **Do, have,** and **be** can act as auxiliary verbs. Modals (**may, can, will,** and so on) are also auxiliary verbs.

> **Do** you have the time?   The car **was** speeding.
> I **have** never been to Italy.   I **may** be late.

base form The form of a verb without any verb endings; the infinitive form without *to.*

> sleep   be   stop

clause A group of words that has a subject and a verb. *See also* **dependent clause** and **main clause.**

> If I leave, ... when he speaks.
> The rain stopped.   . . . that I saw.

common noun A noun that refers to any of a class of people, animals, places, things, or ideas. Common nouns are not capitalized.

> man   cat   city   pencil   grammar

comparative A form of an adjective, adverb, or noun that is used to express differences between two items or situations.

> This book is **heavier than** that one.
> He runs **more quickly than** his brother.
> A CD costs **more money than** a cassette.

complex sentence A sentence that has a main clause and one or more dependent clauses.

> When the bell rang, we were finishing dinner.

compound sentence A sentence that has two main clauses separated by a comma and a conjunction, or by a semi-colon.

> She is very talented; she can sing and dance.

conditional sentence A sentence that expresses a real or unreal situation in the *if* clause, and the (real or unreal) expected result in the main clause.

> If I have time, I will travel to Africa.
> If I had time, I would travel to Africa.

countable noun A common noun that can be counted. It usually has both a singular and a plural form.

> orange — oranges   woman — women

definite article The word **the** in English. It is used to identify nouns based on assumptions about what information the speaker and listener share about the noun. The definite article is also used for making general statements about a whole class or group of nouns.

> Please give me **the** key.
> **The** scorpion is dangerous.

dependent clause A clause that cannot stand alone as a sentence because it depends on the main clause to complete the meaning of the sentence. Also called *subordinate clause.*

> I'm going home **after he calls**.

determiner A word such as **a, an, the, this, that, these, those, my, some, a few,** and **three** that is used before a noun to limit its meaning in some way.

> **those** videos

future A time that is to come. The future is expressed in English with **will, be going to,** the simple present, or the present continuous. These different forms of the future often have different meanings and uses.

> I **will** help you later.
> David **is going to** call later.
> The train **leaves** at 6:05 this evening.
> I**'m driving** to Toronto tomorrow.

gerund An **-ing** form of a verb that is used in place of a noun or pronoun to name an activity or a state.

> **Skiing** is fun.   He doesn't like **being sick**.

if **clause** A dependent clause that begins with **if** and expresses a real or unreal situation.

> **If I have the time,** I'll paint the kitchen.
> **If I had the time,** I'd paint the kitchen.

indefinite article The words **a** and **an** in English. Indefinite articles introduce a noun as a member of a class of nouns or make generalizations about a whole class or group of nouns.

> **An** ocean is **a** large body of water.

independent clause *See* **main clause.**

indirect object A noun or pronoun used after some verbs that refers to the person who receives the direct object of a sentence.

> John wrote a letter to **Mary**.
> Please buy some milk for **us**.

infinitive A verb form that includes **to** + the base form of a verb. An infinitive is used in place of a noun or pronoun to name an activity or situation expressed by a verb.

> Do you like **to swim**?

intransitive verb A verb that cannot be followed by an object.

> We finally **arrived**.

main clause A clause that can be used by itself as a sentence. Also called *independent clause.*

> I'm going home.

main verb A verb that can be used alone in a sentence. A main verb can also occur with an auxiliary verb.

> I **ate** lunch at 11:30.
> Kate can't **eat** lunch today.

modal The auxiliary verbs **can, could, may, might, must, should, will,** and **would.** They modify the meaning of a main verb by expressing ability, authority, formality, politeness, or various degrees of certainty. Also called *modal auxiliary.*

> You **should** take something for your headache.
> Applicants **must** have a high school diploma.

negative statement A sentence with a negative verb.

> I **didn't see** that movie.

noun A word that typically refers to a person, animal, place, thing, or idea.

> Tom   rabbit   store   computer   mathematics

noun clause A dependent clause that can occur in the same place as a noun, pronoun, or noun phrase in a sentence. Noun clauses begin with **wh-** words, **if, whether,** or **that.**

> I don't know **where he is**.
> I wonder **if he's coming**.
> I don't know **whether it's true**.
> I think **that it's a lie**.

noun phrase A phrase formed by a noun and its modifiers. A noun phrase can substitute for a noun in a sentence.

> She drank **milk**.
> She drank **chocolate milk**.
> She drank **the milk**.

object A noun, pronoun, or noun phrase that follows a transitive verb or a preposition.

> He likes **pizza**.   Go with **her**.
> She likes **him**.   Steve threw **the ball**.

passive sentence Passive sentences emphasize the receiver of an action by changing the usual order of the subject and object in a sentence. In the sentence below, the subject **(The letter)** does not perform the action; it receives the action or is the result of an action. The passive is formed with a form of **be** + the past participle of a transitive verb.

> The letter was mailed yesterday.

past continuous A verb form that expresses an action or situation in progress at a specific time in the past. The past continuous is formed with **was** or **were** + verb + **-ing.** Also called *past progressive.*

> A: What **were** you **doing** last night at eight o'clock?
> B: I **was studying**.

past participle A past verb form that may differ from the simple past form of some irregular verbs. It is used to form the present perfect, for example.

> I have never **seen** that movie.

phrasal verb A two- or three-word verb such as **turn down** or **run out of**. The meaning of a phrasal verb is usually different from the meanings of its individual words.

> She **turned down** the job offer.
> Don't **run out of** gas on the freeway.

phrase A group of words that can form a grammatical unit. A phrase can take the form of a noun phrase, verb phrase, adjective phrase, adverbial phrase, or prepositional phrase. This means it can act as a noun, verb, adjective, adverb, or preposition.

> The **tall man** left.   She spoke **too fast**.
> Lee **hit the ball**.   They ran **down the stairs**.

preposition A word such as **at, in, on,** or **to,** that links nouns, pronouns, and gerunds to other words.

prepositional phrase A phrase that consists of a preposition followed by a noun or noun phrase.

> on Sunday   under the table

present continuous A verb form that indicates that an activity is in progress, temporary, or changing. It is formed with **be** + verb + **-ing.** Also called *present progressive*.

> I'm **watering** the garden.
> Ruth **is working** for her uncle.

present perfect A verb form that expresses a connection between the past and the present. It indicates indefinite past time, recent past time, or continuing past time. The present perfect is formed with **have** + the past participle of the main verb.

> I've **seen** that movie.
> The manager **has** just **resigned**.
> We've **been** here for three hours.

pronoun A word that can replace a noun or noun phrase. **I, you, he, she, it, mine,** and **yours** are some examples of pronouns.

quantity expression A word or words that occur before a noun to express a quantity or amount of that noun.

> **a lot of** rain   **few** books   **four** trucks

simple past A verb form that expresses actions and situations that were completed at a definite time in the past.

> Carol **ate** lunch.   She **was** hungry.

simple present A verb form that expresses general statements, especially about habitual or repeated activities and permanent situations.

> Every morning I **catch** the 8:00 bus.
> The earth **is** round.

stative verb A type of verb that is not usually used in the continuous form because it expresses a condition or state that is not changing. **Know, love, see,** and **smell** are some examples.

subject A noun, pronoun, or noun phrase that precedes the verb phrase in a sentence. The subject is closely related to the verb as the doer or experiencer of the action or state, or closely related to the noun that is being described in a sentence with *be*.

> **Erica** kicked the ball.
> **The park** is huge.

subordinate clause *See* **dependent clause.**

superlative A form of an adjective, adverb, or noun that is used to rank an item or situation first or last in a group of three or more.

> This perfume has **the strongest** scent.
> He speaks **the fastest** of all.
> That machine makes **the most noise** of the three.

tense The form of a verb that shows past, present, and future time.

> He **lives** in New York now.
> He **lived** in Washington two years ago.
> He'll **live** in Toronto next year.

time clause A dependent clause that begins with a word such as **while, when, before,** or **after.** It expresses the relationship in time between two different events in the same sentence.

> **Before Sandy left,** she fixed the copy machine.

time expression A phrase that functions as an adverb of time.

> She graduated **three years ago**.
> I'll see them **the day after tomorrow**.

transitive verb A verb that is followed by an object.

> I **read** the book.

uncountable (noncount) noun A common noun that cannot be counted. A noncount noun has no plural form and cannot occur with **a, an,** or a number.

> information   mathematics   weather

verb A word that refers to an action or a state.

> Gina **closed** the window.
> Tim **loves** classical music.

verb phrase A phrase that has a main verb and any objects, adverbs, or dependent clauses that complete the meaning of the verb in the sentence.

> Who **called you**?
> He **walked slowly**.

Appendix IV: **Correlation to *Grammar Sense 1***

EFFECTIVE ACADEMIC WRITING 1: THE PARAGRAPH	GRAMMAR SENSE 1
Unit 2 Using adjectives Using *be* to define and describe	**Chapter 6** Descriptive Adjectives **Chapter 1** Simple Present Statements with *Be*
Unit 3 The simple present	**Chapter 9** The Simple Present
Unit 4 Imperatives Modals of advice, necessity, and prohibition	**Chapter 3** Imperatives **Chapter 22** Modals of Advice, Necessity, and Prohibition
Unit 5 Using *there is/there are* to introduce facts	**Chapter 16** *There Is* and *There Are*
Unit 6 The simple past The past continuous	**Chapter 12** The Simple Past **Chapter 13** The Past Continuous